THE WILTSHIRE REGIMENT
1756-1914
1756-1914

THE WILTSHIRE REGIMENT
1756-1914

MARTIN McINTYRE

TEMPUS

Frontispiece: An officer and colour sergeant of the Duke of Edinburgh's Wiltshire Regiment (62nd & 99th) at Devizes Railway Station, *c.*1887. This railway station became familiar to generations of soldiers from the Wiltshire Regiment who were trained at, demobbed from or posted to the Regimental Depot, Le Marchant Barracks. This print, by the famous Victorian illustrator R. Simkin, was published in the *Army and Navy Gazette* in 1889.

First published 2007

Tempus Publishing
Cirencester Road, Chalford,
Stroud, Gloucestershire, GL6 8PE
www.tempus-publishing.com

Tempus Publishing is an imprint of NPI Media Group

British Library Cataloguing in Publication Data.
A catalogue record for this book is available from the British Library.

ISBN 978 0 7524 4416 1

Typesetting and origination by NPI Media Group
Printed in Great Britain

Contents

The 2nd Battalion Duke of Edinburgh's (Wiltshire) Regiment on parade at Peshawar in 1887. The strength of the battalion at this time was 1,066. Arriving in India during 1882 from South Africa the battalion spent the next six years in the North West Frontier area of India at Rawalpindi, Peshawar, Nowshera, Cherat, Ambala and Mean Meer. In 1891 a two-month march south took the battalion from Amritsar in the Punjab to Jhansi. Two years later came a move to Fort Dufferin in Mandalay, before returning home in 1895. Like all English infantry regiments at that time, a significant number of soldiers came from Ireland with the muster rolls showing names such as O'Driscoll, Murphy and O'Kelly time and again. The travels of infantry battalions at this time were summed up by Kipling:

My name is O'Kelly, I've heard the Revelly
From Birr to Bareilly, from Leeds to Lahore,
Hong-Kong and Peshawur,
Lucknow and Etawah,
And fifty-five more all endin' in 'pore'.
Black Death and his quickness, the depth and the thickness,
Of sorrow and sickness I've known on my way,
But I'm old and I'm nervis,
I'm cast from the Service,
And all I deserve is a shillin' a day.
(Chorus) Shillin' a day,
Bloomin' good pay –
Lucky to touch it, a shillin' a day!

Introduction
and Acknowledgements

Although individuals who served in the Wiltshire Regiment appeared in front of the camera from an early stage, the unit as a whole was not photographed until the mid-1860s. The majority of those photographed during the early years were of officer rank. The long exposure time necessary in the early days of photography meant that it was impossible to take the 'action photos' of combat so familiar in the modern era; most photographers had to be content with posed studies of soldiers in the field with the 'special artist' remaining the pictorial mainstay of action studies until the 1890s. Official photographic archives were not maintained, but some were kept by sergeants' and officers' messes.

In the mid-1930s the compilation of photograph albums was officially sanctioned and the Wiltshire Regiment opened a museum in Le Marchant Barracks, Devizes. Subsequent donations of privately held photograph albums and collections, added to official archives, have resulted in an extensive resource, containing many images that have never previously been published. In 1959 the regiment amalgamated with the Royal Berkshire Regiment to form the Duke of Edinburgh's Royal Regiment (Berkshire and Wiltshire) with a further merger in 1994 producing the Royal Gloucestershire, Berkshire and Wiltshire Regiment. The majority of photographs in this volume are held in the regimental archive at Salisbury and are reproduced with the permission of the Museum Trustees.

This volume covers 1756–1914, with the remainder of the regiment's service up to 1959 in a separate book. Although not designed to be a comprehensive regimental history, a brief synopsis of the regiment's activities is given here, in particular events that led to the wearing of insignia and to nicknames or significant regimental anniversaries.

The 62nd Regiment of Foot began life during the Seven Years' War. In 1756 an urgent Army Order decreed that the fifteen senior Regiments of Foot were each to be enlarged by raising a second battalion. The resulting 2nd/4th Foot was short lived. Two years later a further order made all the recently raised second battalions into separate regiments. Thus the 2nd/4th became the 62nd Regiment of Foot. The new regiment fought in North America, India and the Crimea. At Ferozeshah, on 21 December 1845, the 62nd sustained such heavy casualties among officers that many companies ended up being commanded by sergeants, an event commemorated later by Ferozeshah parades when the Colours were handed over to the sergeants for the day. This traditional parade took place for the last time on 6 December 2006. As a result of a threatened invasion by Napoleon a second battalion – 2nd/62nd – was raised in 1804.

In 1824, the request of the governor of Mauritius for reinforcements was met by raising another new regiment in Glasgow, the 99th (Lanarkshire) Regiment of Foot. After Mauritius, the 99th served in Ireland, Australia, New Zealand, China and South Africa. In 1874 the title of the 99th Foot was changed to that of the Duke of Edinburgh's Regiment, and it was given permission to bear the cypher and coronet of the Duke as its regimental badge. It maintained its association as a lowland regiment, and a diced band was worn on forage caps until 1886. In 1881 the 62nd and 99th Regiments were amalgamated to become the 1st and 2nd Battalions of the Duke of Edinburgh's (Wiltshire) Regiment.

The county of Wiltshire has always produced active volunteer units in the shape of the Militia and Volunteers. The origin of the Wiltshire Militia is somewhat obscure, but it is recorded that the regiment was in existence in 1570, with 1,200 trained men formed into companies. In 1685 they were present at the Battle of Sedgemoor in Monmouth's Rebellion. In 1814 the Wiltshire Militia volunteered for Foreign Service and four officers and 130 other ranks embarked as part of the 2nd Battalion of the Militia Brigade, landing at Bordeaux to serve under Wellington. In 1841 they were awarded the title 'Royal' but gave it up in 1881, when they amalgamated with the regular battalions to become the 3rd (Militia) Battalion of the Duke of Edinburgh's (Wiltshire) Regiment. During the Boer War they served on the island of St Helena as a garrison to guard Boer prisoners. St Helena appears as an honour on their Colours. In 1908 the title 'Militia' was abandoned and the battalion became the 3rd (Special Reserve) Battalion of the Regiment.

In May 1859, when war with France appeared imminent, the government sanctioned the raising of the Rifle Volunteer Corps. The following year the first companies (called Corps) were raised in Salisbury, Trowbridge and Chippenham. In 1861 these were formed into the 1st and 2nd Administration Battalions of the Wiltshire Rifle Volunteers. These subsequently became the 1st Wilts Rifle Volunteers and the 2nd Volunteer Battalion Wiltshire Regiment. In 1900, during the Boer War, a company was recruited from the two Volunteer Battalions as reinforcements to the 2nd Battalion, on active service in South Africa. In 1908, under the Territorial Forces Act, the two Volunteer Battalions were amalgamated into the 4th Battalion Wiltshire Regiment.

All Wiltshire infantry battalions were nicknamed 'The Moonrakers', reflecting the Wiltshire smuggling legend. Individual units gained their own nicknames – the 62nd were, for a short period, called the 'Splashers', referring to the splash marking on the uniform buttons which commemorated the action at Carrickfergus Castle, Ireland, in 1760, when the garrison ran out of ammunition and used buttons instead. They were later known as 'The Springers', attributed to them by General Burgoyne due to their rapidity of movement during the War of American Independence. 'Spring up' was an eighteenth-century light infantry term of command meaning 'advance'. This nickname stayed with the regiment until 1959. A lesser-known and short-lived nickname was 'The Shacks', referring to the shakos worn during the Peninsula War. The 99th were known as 'The Nines', reflecting their regimental number. They were also called the 'The Queen's Pets' because they were always chosen to find the guard on the Royal Pavilion, at Aldershot, in 1858. A more comprehensive account of the regiment's history can be found in *The Story of the Wiltshire Regiment* by Col. N. Kenrick, published in 1963.

Thanks are due to Len Webb and Fred Larimore; also Will Bennett for access to his extensive Wiltshire Regiment collection; museum volunteers include Richard Long-Fox, for his never-ending work on the museum photographic archive and John Peters, the former curator, for his invaluable help on regimental historical matters; Sue Johnson, who has proofread everything and added many useful suggestions; David Chilton, the regimental museum curator for his continuing support, and my wife Carola who has been very supportive and patient over the past few years whilst I carried out this project, and, last but not least, the staff at Tempus Publishing – Amy, Sophie and Stevie – who have helped and guided us through this publishing minefield.

M. McIntyre
The Rifles (Berkshire and Wiltshire) Museum,
The Wardrobe, 58 The Close, Salisbury, Wiltshire, SP1 2EX
Tel +44 (0)1722 419419
www.thewardrobe.org.uk

one

Early Days

The 1st Battalion of the Wiltshire Regiment was raised in 1756 at Torbay at the start of the Seven Years War as a 2nd Battalion of the 4th Foot (later the King's Own Royal Regiment). Recruits were enlisted in most of the south-western counties, Wiltshire furnishing a considerable quota. Its existence was a brief one and, in April 1758, it was given a separate identity as the 62nd Regiment of Foot. This change came as the battalion was at sea, having been drafted to serve as marines under Admiral Boscawen in Canada. Here we see a depiction of a private of the Grenadier Company, 62nd Foot, c.1768. The mitre cap was designed to allow the Grenadier to throw his grenade without knocking off his hat! The regimental museum at Salisbury displays a very good example of this type of headdress. The grenadiers' coat was brick (red) with buff facings.

The harbour of Louisburg on Cape Bereton Island, Canada. In 1758 the 62nd Foot won their first Battle Honour here. The battalion was deployed throughout Admiral Boscawen's fleet as marines and in that capacity took part in the defence of Lighthouse Point (seen to the left of the drawing) together with other actions. The Louisburg Battle Honour was not awarded for 152 years as the War Office stated they had no record of the regiment's participation. The reason for this was that being deployed on-board naval ships the men were on the strength of the Navy not the Army. Three companies of the 62nd later took part in the Battle of Quebec under Gen. Wolfe, but despite half the regiment being present it was never awarded as a Battle Honour.

In 1760 the Regimental Headquarters of the 62nd Foot was situated in Carrickfergus Castle on the northern shore of Belfast Lough. In February of that year, the garrison consisted of nine officers and about 100 new recruits, mainly young Irishmen. A fleet of French men-of-war appeared off the coast, and a force of over 1,000 French troops were landed under the command of the notorious François Thurot, a French privateer. The garrison was outnumbered ten to one with very little ammunition for their muskets. When this ran out they used the buttons off their coats as bullets, and then met their assailants with bricks, stones and bayonets. Although the garrison was eventually overwhelmed, with two men of the 62nd Foot being killed, significant casualties were inflicted on the French.

The 62nd Foot was stationed in Galway, Ireland, when the War of American Independence started in 1775. Sailing for America in April 1776, the regiment's first taste of action was at the Battle of Three Rivers (north-east of Montreal), where it repulsed an American attack. After a move south, the fort of Fort St John was taken. The regiment fought under the command of Gen. Burgoyne, at Saratoga, who is credited with giving them their famous nickname of 'The Springers' because they acted as light infantry. The regiment fought at at Hubertown, Skenesborough, Fort Ann and the Battle of Stillwater 1 (Freeman's Farm) where it lost over 100 men. After their last bayonet charge, when the firing had ceased, Gen. Burgoyne rode up to the 62nd saying 'Well done, my brave Springers'. He knew their losses were heavy, but was not aware that only five officers and sixty men were fit for duty. Here we see three soldiers of the 62nd as they would have appeared during this campaign. In 1804 the 62nd Foot formed a second battalion, the 2nd/62nd, which was later to serve in the Peninsula War.

In 1806 regiments were allowed to choose their own headdress badges, and to wear it on their shako plate with their regiment's number in the centre. The 62nd Foot, at that time in Sicily, adopted the Maltese Cross. One of the reasons given for this choice was that there were six old English families of the name of Wiltshire whose coat of arms or crest included a cross. By 1828 regimental badges had become official and the 62nd's was shown as Maltese Cross within an eight-pointed star. The term 'Maltese Cross', although not strictly correct, was used by the Regiment until 1923 when the proper description 'Cross Patée' was adopted. This regimental postcard showing the glengarry badge was produced by Pte Pearce in the 1920s.

The 2nd/62nd arrived in Spain to join Wellington's Army in October 1813 being placed in Lord Aylmer's brigade (known as 'The Independents'). Their first taste of fighting was in the Pyrenees, with the main action taking place in a wooded area in the grounds of the Mayor of Biarritz at Barrouilhet. The 2nd/62nd captured and lost the house several times. Taking part in several engagements round Bayonne during the course of the siege, over 600 men were lost. The battalion was sent back to Vera, returning several months later to help repulse the last desperate French sortie. Two Battle Honours, Peninsula and Nive, were earned during this campaign, though neither were awarded until some years later. After the war, the 2nd/62nd returned to Ireland. Here we see a sergeant of 2nd/62nd as he would have been equipped during this campaign. He is wearing the shako headress known to the men as 'a shak'. The 2nd/62nd were disbanded in 1817 with 400 men of the battalion joining the 1st/62nd who at that time were in Nova Scotia.

Warminster Company, 1st Battalion Wiltshire Rifle Volunteers, known as the 'The Jolly 10th', in June 1861. At this time, the county of Wiltshire fielded two 1,000-strong Volunteer Battalions and the records show that the life of the battalion was very much connected with the fox-hunting fraternity. The uniform worn at this time was dark green with black lace, similar to that worn by the Rifle Brigade. The headdress badge was two rakes crossed and in the centre, the historic barrel and the moon (this badge was unofficial and was known as the Moonraker's badge). The Volunteers badge went from 'Bugle' to 'Moonraker' and back to 'Bugle', finally ending up in 1908 with the Wiltshire Regiment cross patée cap badge as worn by the regulars.

The Quarter Guard of the 1st Battalion Wiltshire Rifle Volunteers, at Warminster Camp, August 1879. A Wiltshire Volunteer publication at the time included 'Hints to young soldiers' stating:

Nothing is more disgraceful than for a soldier to appear on parade or on duty in a slovenly manner. An awkward position, laughing, talking, or shuffling with hands and feet, have a disagreeable appearance and should be avoided. If a calm attention to the word of command, and a steady eye to the Fugleman is not rigidly observed, it will be impossible for any manoeuvre to be performed with spirit and exactness, which is the very soul of Military Discipline. (The Fugleman carried out the drill movements in front of the squad who would follow his actions.)

It is said that a Wiltshire sentry, being questioned on his duties, replied that he would slope arms to a captain and present arms to the Colonel. 'What would you do if Lt Bouverie came by?' the sentry was asked. 'Lor' bless'ee Zur; I don't take no notice of 'ee, I do know 'im so well.'

The 99th (Lanarkshire) Regiment of Foot sports-day at Cape Town, South Africa in 1868. The regiment had arrived at the Cape of Good Hope early in 1865, after active service in China. Initially, the 99th Foot was divided between Pietermaritzburg, South Africa and the island of St Helena in the Atlantic carrying out garrison duties. The regiment was reunited at the end of 1868 when it was inspected by the Duke of Edinburgh when he visited the Cape. This later led to the 99th receiving the title 'The 99th (Duke of Edinburgh's) Regiment'. In July 1869 they sailed for Portsmouth in the troopship *Orontes*.

B Company, 99th Foot, Cape Town, South Africa, in 1868. It is believed that this photograph was taken during HRH the Duke of Edinburgh's visit to the regiment. The soldiers wearing the white jackets are bandsmen. It was during this posting that the regiment had their first Kneller Hall trained bandmaster (Kneller Hall is the Army School of Music). In 1870 an application by the 99th Foot to have three pipers on the battalion strength, as permitted in other Scottish regiments, was turned down.

The 99th Foot was stationed in Cape Town from 1865 to 1869. During that time it was responsible for providing the garrison on the island of St Helena in the Atlantic. Companies F, G, H and I arrived there on 19 May 1867. Here we see the nine officers who went with those companies: Maj. Ely, Capts Gray, Day and Stewart, Ensigns Kennedy, Cooch, Blaxland, Banfather and Macklin. These officers are wearing diced bands around their caps, authorised only two months earlier to signify their designation as a Lowland Regiment.

The officers of the 99th Foot, Cape Town, South Africa, c.1868. At this time the regiment was under the command of Lt-Col. John Hart Dunne, who had taken over in 1865. He remained in command until 1877. In this photograph is Maj. Welman who later returned to the Cape in 1879 as the Commanding Officer of the 99th Foot during the Zulu War. No doubt the knowledge he gained about this area stood him in good stead in that later campaign.

Sgt-Maj. Ball and the Sergeants' Mess members, 62nd Foot, Ireland, c.1867. The battalion moved to Ireland in 1866 spending two years in the area of Cork which is where this photograph was taken. It was deployed during this time to deal with the Fenian troubles. The photograph is of interest as it is the only example we have of the drum major wearing a bearskin.

Sgt-Maj. Ball and the remainder of his Sergeants' Mess, Ireland, 1867. Sgt-Maj. Ball is seated in the centre with four chevrons and a crown indicating his rank. The colour sergeants have a single chevron with crossed flags over. The band sergeant is wearing a white tunic. The man to the right, in civilian clothes, is probably a canteen manager, recruited from the ranks of ex-Non-Commissioned Officers. At the end of 1868 the 62nd Foot sailed for India where they were to suffer dreadfully from the effects of cholera.

Members of the Wiltshire Rifle Volunteers Corps together with two members of the 20th Foot (East Devon's) – later Lancashire Fusiliers – at a shooting match in 1868. The weapons are Enfield percussion rifles, at least two of which have been converted with the new Snider breech-loading device. The venue is believed to be Semington near Melksham, Wiltshire.

The 62nd (Wiltshire) Regiment of Foot, Lucknow in 1869. Standing, left to right: Capt. Theobald, Lt Knox, Ens. J. Carthew, Lt-Adj. T. Forsyth, Lt Gamble (QM) (fought at Ferozeshah, Sobraon and in the Crimea), Capts Cubitt, Gream and Wodehouse (Instructor of Musketry), Ensigns Forest, Arthur, Williams and Hayne, Lts Poole and Todd, Sgt-Maj. Hollingsworth, Lt Rogers, Capt. Frazer, Ens. Lewis, Capt. Kelly, Lt A. Goding and -?-. Sitting: Paymaster J. Minchin, Mrs Fitzsimon, Capt. Fitzsimon, Miss Gamble, Capt. Dundas, Mrs MacWhirter, Mrs Dundas, Mrs Kelly, Mrs Reade and Capt. Reade. Front row: Ensigns Carter, Hingston and MacWhirter.

Lt Carter later commanded the 2nd Battalion during the Boer War and became a regimental historian with the results of his work being used to this day. The 62nd Foot served in India from 1868 to 1880 then went to Aden.

On 27 April 1874 the 99th Foot received a letter from the War Office:

> I have the honour, by desire of H.R.H., the Field Marshal Commanding in Chief, to acquaint you that Her Majesty has been graciously pleased to approve of the 99th Regiment being in future styled the 99th (Duke of Edinburgh's) Regiment, and of its bearing on its second, or Regimental Colour, His Royal Highness's Coronet and Cypher.

So began an association with this title that was to last to 1959 and beyond into the amalgamated regiment, The Duke of Edinburgh's Royal Regiment (Berkshire and Wiltshire). This image shows a regimentally produced postcard by Pte Pearce. Note the thistles surrounding the Duke of Edinburgh's cypher, signifying the Scottish origins of the 99th Foot.

The sergeants of the 99th Foot at the Curragh Camp, Ireland, c.1875. The regiment arrived in Ireland in August 1875, where the new Martini-Henry rifles were immediately issued, followed by a series of musketry exercises to familiarise the men with the new weapon. The only identifiable soldier in this photograph is Col-Sgt Davis (front row, third from right) The regiment left Ireland in February 1878, going to Chatham where it remained until deployed on active service in the Zulu War in 1879.

The band of the 99th Foot, Rawalpindi, India, c.1883. The 99th arrived in India in 1882 after active service against the Zulus. The band members wearing the Zulu War medals would have been with the besieged garrison at Eshowe in South Africa, where they played regular concerts together with the band of the Buffs to help keep the troops' morale high. The only identified soldiers in this photo are Cpl J. Box (left, standing with the double bass), Sgt H.J. Cook (seated, fifth from left) and G. Bates, bandmaster (sixth from left). To the right of the bass drum is Capt. & Adj. H. Harford. Capt. Harford was a Zulu War veteran who wrote a journal of his adventures in Natal, which was published in South Africa in 1978.

The band of the 11th Wiltshire Volunteer Rifle Corps (later F and G Companies of the 2nd Volunteer Battalion) taken about 1879/80, outside the Mechanics Institute in New Swindon. The bearded man wearing the medals (second row from the back, third from right) was an ex-regular Crimean War veteran called McCaffrey. Many of these men were also members of their local town or village bands, which were widespread in Wiltshire at that time.

The ambulance wagon of the 2nd Volunteer Battalion, believed to have been taken at Calne in the late 1890s. The strength of this battalion in 1893 was 1,090 officers and men. Their uniform at this time was very much based on that worn by Rifle Regiments and consisted of a black braided tunic, a busby with plume and a cross-belt with silver plate and chains for officers and bronze for other ranks.

The first team of the shooting club of F and G (Swindon) Companies, 2nd Volunteer Battalion, pictured here in 1896. The photograph was marked 'Adieu Martini-Henry', probably meaning that the Wiltshire Volunteers were about to say farewell to their Martini-Henry rifles shown in the photograph, before being equipped with the Lee-Metford rifle. Rear row, left to right: Acting Sgt Westcott, Col-Sgt Osborne, Cpl Nugent, L/Sgt Clarke, L/Cpl Gardiner, Cpl Ball, Honorary Member Clissold and Pte Jones. Sitting: Pte Wager, Sgt Smith, Sgt Taylor, L/Cpl Haines and L/Cpl Jones.

two

Victoria's Wars

In 1845 the 62nd Foot took part in the First Sikh War. At the Battle of Ferozeshah, 21 December, the 62nd attacked the Sikh positions, losing eighteen officers killed or wounded. The regiment was awarded the Battle Honour Ferozeshah. Sgt Sanderson later remembered, 'In those days a sergeant used to precede the colour party by about ten paces to maintain the true direction. I was the directing sergeant of the regiment.' He went on to say 'the colour party suffered terribly, no less than four officers being put *hors de combat*, the centre sergeant, then orderly-room clerk, later Colonel William Dring, being wounded by grapeshot. The colours were brought out of action by two sergeants.' By that evening Sgt Sanderson commanded a company. He was later commissioned and was the only officer of the 62nd to become a Military Knight of Windsor. This representation of the battle was commissioned by the regiment in the 1980s.

Sgt William Humphries, 62nd Foot, who fought, and was wounded, at the Battle of Ferozeshah. He was born in Essex and joined the 62nd Foot in 1834, serving for a total of fourteen years, of which thirteen years 132 days were spent abroad in the East Indies. He was granted a bounty of 6*d* per day for his gallant conduct at Ferozeshah. Later in life he became a regular visitor to the 1st Battalion. It was recorded:

The enemy's fire increased to a storm of grape and canister and within that space seven officers were killed and eleven wounded, ninety-seven non-commissioned officers and privates fell killed and 184 wounded. Lieutenant Gubbins fell from sabre cuts in advance of his company, Lieutenant Kelly fell from sabre cuts close to the entrenchments and the following men distinguished themselves at the same place, Sergeant Humphries received a sabre cut, Lance Corporal Floveritt wounded on his left hand, Pte Short, across the head, and Private Westcott across the back.

Depicted here is the second day of the Battle of Ferozeshah, by which time the 62nd Foot had only six officers left, including Maj. Shortt who, though wounded, still led the regiment. When the Sikhs retreated, the 62nd was sent ahead with most of its companies commanded by sergeants. The action continued until 3 p.m. The low number of British casualties in this close quarter situation was attributed to the Sikhs firing their weapons from the hip. The 62nd Foot went on to fight at the battles of Aliwal and Sobraon. At Sobraon, Capt. William Mathias was described as follows, 'He wore a shell-jacket, black serge trousers, covered in blood stains from Aliwal, carrying the sword taken from a Sikh gunner and a couple of pistols in his belt, with a puggerie wound round his forage cap as a protection from the sun'.

A modern photograph of the Anglo-Indian memorial. It stands in a very rural setting, not far from the village of Ferozeshah. About 35ft in height, built of brick, it is now in a state of some disrepair. The base has the word Ferozeshah in English on one side, an inscription in Jawi on the second side, with the third side blank. The regiment commemorated this battle on or near 21 December every year, but did not formally mark the date until the late 1890s. The tradition of handing the Colours to the sergeants as a reminder of the time when the sergeants commanded most of the companies was not introduced until 1921, when the 1st Battalion was stationed in Ireland. Lt-Col. Rowan initially formalised the parade, which was further developed by Lt-Col. Kenrick. After the amalgamation in 1959, the tradition was carried over into the Duke of Edinburgh's Royal Regiment and later still into the Royal Gloucestershire, Berkshire and Wiltshire Regiment. In 2007 the regiment became part of the 1st Battalion of the Rifles, the Battle Honour Ferozeshah is displayed on the cross-belt badge.

Above left: In the same year that the 62nd were in action against the Sikhs, the 99th Foot were engaged on the other side of the globe in New Zealand in the First Maori War – now referred to as the Land Wars. Trouble between the Maoris and the settlers over land rights and the imposition of customs duties led to a rebellion. Seen here is Honi Heke Pokai of the Ngaputi who was responsible for starting what was later referred to as the Flagstaff War, when he chopped down the flagstaff at Maiki Hill. The flank companies of the 99th Foot were sent from Australia to reinforce the British garrison. They arrived in June 1845 with Lt-Col. Despard in command. Maj. McPherson commanded the Grenadier Company and the 99th detachment, with Lt Johnson commanding the Light Company. Lt-Col. Despard was in overall command of the British expedition.

Above right: Maj. McPherson, 99th Foot. He joined the regiment on its formation in 1824 having had previous service in the 78th Foot with which he served in Holland, including the actions at Merxem and the bombardment of Antwerp. He commanded the Grenadier Company of the 99th and went with it in 1845 to New Zealand, to take part in the suppression of the Maori rebellion. Known to his men as 'The Jolly Old Major' he played a prominent part in the assault on the Ohaeawai Pa. Lt Beatty of the 99th led the storming party, otherwise known as 'the Forlorn Hope', followed by the principal attacking party under the command of Maj. McPherson. One of his officers, Ensign Blackburn, later recalled:

> The men gave three cheers and rushed forward, they soon reached the Pa, not a shot was fired on either side till the troops were touching the Pa, but then the enemy opened fire, which they had reserved till this moment, and sent our front ranks reeling back and many a gallant spirit to eternity. [Our men] tore down the outer fencing of green flax and exposed the second fence of large palisades strongly driven into the ground and firmly lashed together, they searched in vain for a breach and not finding any, commenced pulling at them with their bare hands.

Maj. McPherson was badly wounded in the unsuccessful attack.

Right: Lt Patrick Johnson, 99th Foot. He joined the regiment in 1839 and went with it to Australia. He was there when the First Maori War started and was one of the officers selected to go to New Zealand. He commanded the Light Company throughout the campaign and was slightly wounded in the attack at Ohaeawai Pa. Ensign Blackburn, who was later killed in New Zealand, wrote in his diary, 'Pat Johnson received a slanting ball on his forehead and he was saved by the peak of his cap, and so he only received slight concussion.' Lt Johnson became the adjutant of the 99th Foot in 1851.

The soldiers of the 99th fought at Ohaeawai Pa, Pukatutu's Pa and in the Valley of the Hutt, and were stationed in Hobart from 1848 to 1856. Many veterans settled in New Zealand. Here we see the last four surviving old soldiers, left to right: George Clarke, Richard Shea, A. Crowhurst and Wilson. Pte Shea was convicted of striking Lt Johnson at Porirua and transported for life, which meant he could not return to the United Kingdom. They are seen here in front of the war memorial in Hobart, Tasmania, which commemorates twenty-four men of the regiment who were killed on active service in the New Zealand Maori Wars of 1845–46. The memorial, the first to be built in Australia, was erected in 1850 and was paid for by voluntary subscriptions from officers and men of the regiment.

Above left: The 62nd Foot landed in the Crimea on 13 November 1854, just after the Battle of Inkerman, and spent the worst Russian winter for 100 years on the heights before Sevastopol. At the assault on the Great Redan, Sevastopol, 8 September 1856, the British storming party was provided by the 41st and 62nd of Foot in equal numbers. The 62nd's party consisted of twelve officers and 245 rank and file. During the advance under heavy enemy fire and the hand to hand battle that followed, the 62nd lost half their number and were highly commended for their courage in the assault, with twenty-five of all ranks Mentioned in Dispatches, more than any other regiment taking part. Here we see Col. Cooch, in the uniform of Her Majesty's bodyguard. He fought at the Quarries and the Great Redan, receiving a Brevet Majority for the latter, and being recommended for the Victoria Cross. Mentioned in the dispatches of Gen. Sir James Simpson, GCB, he was awarded the Sardinian War Medal for long service in the trenches before Sevastopol.

Above right: Sgt-Maj. Charles Ball, 62nd of Foot, a veteran of the Crimean War pictured here in Ireland in 1867. He was born in 1829 and enlisted into the regiment in 1847. His early service was in England, which included mounting guard at Windsor Castle when the 62nd Foot replaced the 2nd Coldstream who were on riot duty in London. He later served with the regiment in Ireland, Malta, Crimea and Nova Scotia, before returning in 1866 to Ireland. In 1869 he was discharged to pension, becoming a 1st Class Sergeant Instructor with the 1st Manchester Rifle Volunteers until 1885. His total service in the regular army was twenty-one years and 343 days, and with the Volunteers, fifteen years and 239 days, giving him a total military service of thirty-seven years and 217 days. He received the Crimea Campaign Medal with clasp Sevastopol, the Turkish Medal and Good Conduct Medal with gratuity of £15 for long service and good conduct.

Opposite below: Officers of the 99th, China, 1860-61. Left to right: QM John Johnston, Capt. Charles Burton, Paymaster Frank Potter, Lt-Col. Henry James Day (Commanding Officer), -?-, and Ensign John Francis Stephens. After returning to Hong Kong the Light Company was sent to Shanghai under Capt. Burton, where it fought the Taiping rebels in the assault on the rebel camp at Tserpoo on 17 April 1862.

Above: In February 1860, the 99th Foot sailed from Calcutta to join an expedition going to North China. They arrived at Hong Kong in March and went north to Chusan. Here we see the area of the tented camp of the 99th Foot, which was described by one of the officers, Capt. Townsend, as:

> A long range of mountains stretched across the northern horizon, and these were covered with snow, making us, who were lightly clad, shiver, and dress ourselves in all the furs and padded silk garments we could lay hold of. The farm houses in which some of us were living, others being in tents, were warm and dirty.

The 99th remained on garrison duties until the advance on Pekin (Peking) in September 1860.

The 99th Foot in action on the advance to Pekin which commenced on 8 September 1860. The regiment was the advance guard to the Anglo-French Army and bodyguard to Lord Elgin. Within a week they reached the town of Hosiwoo, twenty miles from Pekin. Their first major action against the Tarters came at Chang-Chai-Wan.

On 18 September 1860, together with the 1st King's Dragoon Guards, the 99th Foot mounted a successful attack against an enemy stronghold at Chang-Chai-Wan, only a short distance from Pekin. The advance to Pekin then continued and by nightfall the suburbs of the city had been reached. The 99th were fairly comfortable in the area of Pu-Se-Tsa, except for one man who received twenty-four strokes of the cat on the spot for impudence to the Provost Marshal. With the harsh discipline of the time, this was universally regarded as a good practical joke. It was at this point that the French Army, awakened by an early reveille, rose and quietly entered Pekin city to commence their looting, leaving the British still sleeping.

The plundering of the Yuen Ming Yuen (otherwise known as the Summer Palace) in Pekin was described in the regimental magazine *The Nines* by one of those present. He wrote:

It had been well looted by the French and by some of our cavalry before some of The Nines and myself got a chance at it, and when we did we had to give up all our loot, which was sold by auction and fetched a large sum, the share of the subaltern being about £36. By the way, when speaking of the Summer Palace, I forgot to advise all looters to carry about with them a small bottle of gold testing fluid. Many of us had noticed a large model of a pagoda, and had passed it by thinking it to be brass, but an officer of Sikhs, who had got his experience at the sack of Delhi, thought otherwise, and found it to be gold. He sold it to the Oriental Bank in Hong Kong for £7,000.

Independent looting by soldiers would result in the lash; organised looting was a different matter. The author, using the pseudonym 'Induna', was Capt. Horace Townshend of the 99th Foot, who served in the regiment from 1857 to 1865. He is pictured here with his wife in retirement in Cork.

Three companies of the 99th Foot were billeted in this Joss House. It was described by John Hart Dunne, later Colonel of the Regiment, in his book *From Calcutta to Pekin*. 'My company together with two others are in a Joss house, and the remaining companies are distributed all over the town. Our Joss House is about the best I have seen. You enter under a gate, with large stone dragons over it, into a small courtyard, through which you pass into a hall, with two immense figures on each side.' Here we see some soldiers of the 99th resting on the porch.

This is believed to be another view of the same set of buildings within the Joss House complex. Capt. Hart Dunne wrote, 'This is the quarter of the Grenadier Company, of the 99th, and the effect of seeing soldiers' beds with belts and fire-locks, amongst all these outlandish beings, is somewhat odd.' These temporary barracks were a luxury, the 99th spent most of this campaign either under canvas or in the open.

As well as the expected kind of plunder from the Palace complex, such as gold, silks and jades, there were several small dogs. One, later appropriately named 'Looty', was acquired by Capt. Hart Dunne of the 99th. He described it as 'a pretty little dog, smaller than any King Charles... It has silver bells round its neck, and people say it is the most perfect little beauty they ever saw.' Capt. Hart Dunne presented Looty to Queen Victoria. The dog was painted by Frederick William Keyl, the pupil of Sir Edwin Landseer, who produced numerous animal studies for the Queen.

Five valuable china vases taken from the Emperor's Summer Palace in Pekin by the 99th Foot.
These vases suffered over the following years from the battalion's travels throughout the world. The
design on two of them depicts a Mongolian horse farm, the other three are incense burners whose
tops were missing when they were taken from the palace. These vases are now on display in the
regimental museum in Salisbury, Wiltshire.

Remains of the Yuen Ming Yuen (Summer Palace), Pekin. Because of the violation of the flag of
truce and the outrageous treatment of prisoners, the Summer Palace was selected for retribution.
The work of destruction – later criticized as a mistaken vengeance – was carried out by British
troops and for two days the smoke of the burning buildings hung like a pall in the skies. In
spite of strict prohibitions against looting, the Allied soldiers, maddened by the murder of their
comrades, carried away most of what was portable, the gold plates from temple ceilings, golden
images from the altars, jades and pearls. The regimental history recorded, 'So ended a war that was
occasionally dangerous but often lucrative.'

In 1878 the 99th Foot was stationed in Chatham, Kent, and it was from there that it sailed for South Africa as part of the expedition against the Zulus and their Chief Cetshwayo. For some years there had been trouble over the border between Zululand, and the Transvaal and Natal. Because Cetshwayo failed to respond to a demand for better control and behaviour, an expedition was mounted. Here we see a regimental postcard produced by the 99th Foot prior to this campaign in Natal. This image clearly shows the frame of mind that existed at the time when the 'redcoat' went to fight the 'savages' on the African continent. The reality proved to be somewhat different.

Col-Sgt J.W. Burnett of the 99th Foot, pictured here after his return from the Zulu Wars. His view of the Zulus was altered after seeing them in action and this was reflected in a letter he wrote home after the battle at Inyezane, reminding a friend how they used to joke about fighting Africans. He now saw things differently:

> I never thought [Africans] would make such a stand. They came on with utter disregard of danger … our 'school' at Chatham, over one hot whiskey, used to laugh about these [Africans], but I assure you that fighting with them was terribly earnest work and not child's play.

An *Illustrated London News* engraving showing Headquarters Company of the 99th Foot with the Commanding Officer Lt-Col. Welman and F and H Companies boarding the SS *Asiatic* en route to South Africa, December 1878. This ship embarked 300 officers and men, besides women and children. The telegram received by the 99th Foot at Chatham on 25 November 1878 read: 'Hold ninety-ninth foot in readiness to embark at the shortest notice for Natal and telegraph tomorrow morning the number of soldiers wives and children requiring conveyance and if possible the officers'. They landed at Durban in January 1879.

Lt-Col. William Henry Dowling Reeves Welman, CB, the Commanding Officer of the 99th Foot during the Zulu Campaign. He joined the 99th in 1847 and served in the regiment for many years, including the Cape in 1865. On arrival in South Africa in 1879 he left two companies to garrison Durban and Stanger, taking the remainder of the regiment to the 1st Division concentration area on the Lower Tugela River. He commanded the second section of Col. Pearson's column. He then spent the next two months besieged in Eshowe. After the campaign he went to Bermuda and in 1882 he took the regiment to India, relinquishing command in Deolali. After thirty-four years, service in the regiment, he retired as a major-general. (Col. Pearson of the Buffs started his army career in the 99th before exchanging into the 3rd Foot.)

A Company of the 99th Foot crosses the Tugela River on a pont at the start of the invasion of Zululand, 12 January 1879. The 99th Foot formed part of No.1 Column under the command of Col. Pearson. The working of the pont, a flat bottomed vessel, some 30ft long by eleven broad, attached to a cable, was found satisfactory. It was hauled across by oxen and two to three trips per hour were made. By the evening of the 12 January 1879 all of the 3rd Foot (Buffs) and most of the 99th Foot were safety across and encamped on the Zulu side of the river.

The camp of No.1 Column, 15 January 1879, on the Zulu side of the Tugela River prior to the advance. The tents of the 99th are on the right, with the Buffs in the centre and the Naval Brigade and Royal Engineers on the left. The 99th Foot consisted of six companies under the command of Lt-Col. Welman. No.1 Column advanced in two sections with the first under the command of Col. Pearson and the second under Lt-Col. Welman. Their first obstacle was the Amatikulu River.

An *Illustrated London News* engraving depicting the rearguard of the 99th Regiment crossing the Amatikulu River, 21 January 1879. This is on the opposite bank to Fort Crealock. Lt-Col. Welman's oxen column consisted of eighty wagons. Before they could cross this river a working party was sent forward to improve the approaches to the ford, this was completed with the party returning that evening. Most of the companies were deployed to provide protection for this very long wagon train which was extremely vulnerable to Zulu attack.

This is believed to be a photograph of the same location with the photographer standing on the same side of the river. The banks have been cut back to widen the track by the local labour, who are sitting by the side of the track. The Amatikulu River, though rather deep, was fordable and was passed without much difficulty. The column had one sharp action against the Zulus at Inyezane. The brunt of that action was taken by the Buffs with the 99th in support; Zulu casualties were estimated at 300. The column then made its way to the Mission Station at Eshowe.

On the morning of 24 January, the column occupied the Mission Station at Eshowe without opposition. The mission buildings, though deserted for many months, were not in bad repair and steps were taken to fortify them. The two companies of the 99th, including the band, worked very hard to ensure that the defences, part of which can be seen here, were substantial enough to withstand any attack by the Zulus. A soldier later remembered:

> From that time up to, I may say, January 30th we had to work almost day and night
> ... and we have at last got it completed. It is a massive looking work, and can afford
> shelter to all the troops. The moat no Zulu can get over, and I should venture to
> say that, arranged as it now is, the whole Zulu force would fail to get an entrance,
> although we only number 400 men.

The garrison was provided by soldiers of the 99th Foot and the Buffs. The Zulu commanders were wise enough to know that an attack on this type of fortified location would result in substantial casualties, and so never attacked it. Instead they surrounded the Mission Station, largely confining its occupants. This photograph, taken after the relief column arrived, shows the Mission Station buildings. They were destroyed by the Zulus after the British left.

During the siege Lt H.W. Rowden formed an irregular horse together with some men of the Alexandria Mounted Rifles. This group was used for vedettes and raiding and caused considerable problems for the Zulus. Lt Rowden was Mentioned in Dispatches twice. The first read, 'young Rowden, 99th Regiment, has proved himself most useful as head of our mounted scouts, he and his men are most vigilant'. The second read, 'By day the picquet duties were performed by a small vedette corps, formed by a few men of the Mounted Infantry, and Natal Volunteers, as organised by Lt. Rowden, 99th Regiment and Capt. Shervinton, Native Contingent. These vedettes were constantly under fire.' (Capt. Shervinton was later recommended for the Victoria Cross for rescuing Pte Brooks of the 99th from the Zulus.) Rowden was a good polo player and was very keen on trying to keep his men from drinking and smoking. He retired to Oxford where he threw himself into local church affairs and was instrumental in helping to form the Parish of St Andrew, Oxford, in 1906. He died in 1921.

On 1 March 1879, 400 men from the besieged garrison raided the Kraal of Prince Dabulamanzi. This raiding party included a company of the 99th Foot and mounted men under the command of Lt Rowden. The raiders were spotted by the Zulus, who subsequently fled. Lt Rowden and fifteen of his men rode ahead and burned down sixty-two huts. The raid was a total success, carried out with no casualties. Here we see an *Illustrated London News* engraving depicting the raid. The raiding party then returned to the Mission Station to await the relief column. It is said that Prince Dabulamanzi became aware of Lt Rowden's action on this raid and marked his future movements, determined to kill him, but was unsuccessful.

One of the mounted infantry soldiers under the command of Lt Rowden was Pte Carson, 99th Foot. Like all members of this small unit he was constantly engaged on vedette duties. On 7 March 1879 he was seriously wounded when he was ambushed by Zulus. Despite his wounds he managed to gallop back to his fellow vedettes and then return to the fort, where two of his fingers were amputated. This Victorian illustration incorrectly shows Pte Carson fending off the Zulus with his rifle; in fact it remained across his back throughout the action. Ten days later Pte W. Kent was not so lucky; his horse was shot and wounded. It reared up and threw him off and he died under a flurry of assegai stabs. When his body was recovered it was discovered that he had eighteen wounds. After that it was decided that infantry should sweep the outlying area each morning before the vedettes were posted.

Pte Carson, pictured here later in life while working as a hotel porter in Belfast. After the attack referred to above he was immediately promoted to lance corporal, eventually retiring as a sergeant. The regimental magazine *The Nines* later told his story:

> One of the Vedettes, Pte Carson attached to the Mounted Infantry, went out to patrol. Some eleven Zulus sprang out of the long grass and seized the horse by the mane; he at once stuck his spurs in and got clear of them. They then fired at him, one bullet taking off two fingers of one of his hands, a second struck him on the left thigh, passed through it, then through the pommel of the saddle and into the other leg, a third went through his right arm, a fourth struck his rifle which was slung over his back. His horse was also assegaied on the flank.

He accounted for the Zulus' bad shooting by them holding out their rifles at full arms length. The injuries received by Pte Carson are clear to see in this photograph which shows the hand with the missing fingers.

The relief column en route to Eshowe paused at Gingindlovu★ and formed a square with the five companies of the 99th Foot positioned on its west face. At 5.45 a.m. the piquets reported that the Zulus were approaching. Very little preparation was needed as all of the troops were at their posts. The Zulus first assaulted the north face of the square then moved round to the west face where they attacked the 99th. Lt Johnson was killed at this point. The assault lasted for an hour and a half with three sides of the square being attacked. This *Illustrated London News* engraving shows the final repulse of the Zulus by Maj. Barrow's mounted infantry, whose freshly issued sabres caused many casualties amongst the Zulus. This mounted unit included soldiers of the 99th. The British later estimated that they were attacked by five Zulu regiments amounting to 11,000 men. British casualties were nine killed and fifty-two wounded, four of whom died later. The 99th lost one officer (Lt Johnson) and two men (Pte Smith and Pte Lawrence). After the battle the Mission Station was relieved. Both Pte Smith and Pte Lawrence are buried at Gingindlovu, but their graves mistakenly show them as serving in the 91st Foot. ★[Gingindlovu – 'The place of he who swallowed the elephant'. The soldiers, unable to master the Zulu language, called it 'gin, gin, I love you'.]

Lt George Charles Jefferyes Johnson, 99th Foot. Born in Cork and educated at Cheltenham College he joined the 99th at Shorncliffe after passing out of Sandhurst in 1872. This was followed by postings to the Curragh and Chatham. During this time he passed a course in musketry at Hythe leaving with a first class certificate. He was appointed as a Instructor of Musketry to the regiment, an appointment he held at his death. Going with the regiment to Natal he was present at the Battle of Inyezane, where his colour sergeant was shot at his side. He commanded Fort Pearson for six weeks. He then commanded his company on the column to relieve Eshowe and was with his company at Gingindlovu forming part of the outlying piquets when they first sighted the attacking Zulu Army. Because he was a skilled marksman he had taken a rifle from one of his men to try and deal with a Zulu who was 'doing much mischief'. He had fired several times, when suddenly placing his hand to his breast, he exclaimed 'I am shot' and died ten minutes later. He was buried at Gingindlovu and is commemorated in Cork Cathedral and Chatham church.

The Eshowe Mission Station was relieved on 3 April 1879 after the successful battle at Gingindlovu, but this proved too be to late for the subject of this portrait. Lt & Adj. Arthur Stewart Fielding Davison had entered Sandhurst in 1874, passing out with a first class certificate. He was commissioned into the 99th Foot, joining the regiment at the Curragh, Ireland, later serving at Kilkenny and Templemore. In November 1878, while at Chatham, he received the appointment of adjutant, and the next month went with the regiment to Natal and proceeded to the Lower Tugela Drift, taking part in the advance of Col. Pearson's column to Eshowe. He was present at the Battle of Inyezane on the morning of 22 January, and the subsequent occupation of Eshowe. In March he was struck down with typhoid fever, dying on 27 March 1879, a week before the besieged garrison was relieved. He was buried at Eshowe.

The graveyard at Eshowe, the last resting place for the thirty-one soldiers who died during the siege, which lasted from 24 January to 3 April 1879. In addition to Lt Davison, the following soldiers of the 9th Foot were also buried here: Ptes Shields and Paul (dysentery), Ptes Lewis, Roden, Swann and Venn (enteric fever), Ptes Coombes (typhoid fever), Tubb (sunstroke), Knee (drowned) and Kent (killed by Zulus).

Prince Dabulamanzi (centre) was King Cetshwayo's half-brother and the commander of the iNdluyengwe regiment. He was well known to the soldiers of the 99th Foot. He commanded the Zulu reserve at Isandlwana and played a significant part at Rorke's Drift. He was in command of some of the Zulu forces that besieged the 99th at Eshowe, and he fought at Gingindlovu as a subordinate to Somopho KaZikala the senior Zulu commander.

The cemetery at Euphorbia Hill, Fort Pearson, is largely filled by those who died from disease rather than enemy action. Soldiers from the 99th Foot known to be buried here are: Ptes C. Baden (died 2 March 1879), N. Jones (3 March 1879) and W. Painter (13 March 1879). All three were in D Company and died from typhoid. The regiment's losses in Natal were three officers: Lt Davison and 2nd-Lt D'Arcy (disease), and Lt Johnson (killed in action); and forty-two NCOs and men. Of these only four were killed in action, the others dying from abscess on liver (one), alcoholic poisoning (one), sunstroke (one), drowning (two) and disease (thirty-three). Also sent home on account of illness were seven officers and 101 men. After the campaign, the regiment made its way to Bermuda calling in at St Helena to pick up the garrison of two officers, five NCOs, a drummer, sixty-seven privates, three women and five children there. A draft of 113 NCOs and men were sent to join the 62nd (Wiltshire) Foot in India.

The officers' mess, 99th Foot, Bermuda, 1881. The regiment arrived at this camp in February 1880 after arduous active service against the Zulus in Natal. The spoils of war in the shape of the Zulu war shields and assegais are on display and were for a number of years afterwards. Today many of these can be seen in the regimental museum in Salisbury, Wiltshire. The shield in the centre is the large isihlangu shield and the one to the right is the smaller umbumbuluzo war shield introduced by Cetshwayo in the 1850s, together with a selection of stabbing and throwing spears.

The 99th Foot on parade, Prospect Camp, Bermuda, 1881. In March 1881 the regiment was due to move to Barbados for garrison duties but this was changed at the last moment. The order to return to Africa was announced whilst the regiment was drawn up on the parade ground at Prospect Camp with the intention of being photographed. It was not well received until Col. Walker made it clear it was for active service (First Boer War). He waved his sword over his head and said, 'Boys we are off for the Cape.' Three prolonged cheers were at once given by the men. The war finished before they arrived, and the 99th Foot was to see no further active service until the Boer War in 1899.

three

March on the
Colours

The remains of the King's Colour of the 62nd Foot, returned to the regiment in 1927 by the Royal United Service Institution. The Colour came from the Tower of London. An investigation carried out at that time established that it was in the possession of the regiment in 1772 and had been stripped from its staff and hidden in 1777 after the battle of Saratoga, during the War of American Independence. In 1780 some officers of the 62nd who had been taken prisoner by the Americans were exchanged and returned home. This King's Colour was probably smuggled back to England at that time.

The only known photograph of the Regimental Colour of the 99th Foot. The Colours were returned in Glasgow on the formation of the regiment in 1824 by the Colonel of the Regiment, Maj.-Gen. Gage John Hall. They were carried for the first twelve years on the Island of Mauritius. In 1841 they were replaced by Colours presented at Chatham by Miss Douglas, the daughter of the Colonel of the Regiment, Lt-Gen. Sir Howard Douglas. The old Colours were laid up in St Giles's church, Edinburgh, and were removed to the regimental museum, in the late 1970s.

The 99th Foot in Natal, South Africa, 1865. To the left the bandsmen are wearing white tunics. The Colours shown here were presented at Chatham on 20 October 1841 and were carried by the regiment in Australia and China during 1860. They were replaced in 1871, but remained in the possession of the regiment until 1874, when they were handed over to the Duke of Edinburgh. It was not all parades for the 99th – on 5 July 1865, seven officers and 178 other ranks marched from Fort Napier to Ladysmith (100 miles) to assist the Civil Authorities against dissident Basutos. This photograph was presented to the regiment in 1938 by the son of the late General Sir John Hart Dunne, Colonel of the Regiment from 1898 to 1924.

HRH Prince Alfred, Duke of Edinburgh. In 1868, the 99th Foot were reunited at Cape Town having previously been divided between Pietermaritzburg in South Africa and the island of St Helena. The Duke of Edinburgh, at his own request, inspected the regiment in Cape Town, starting an association that lasted until his death. Whilst at Cape Town he promised the regiment that he would present them with new colours, a promise honoured in 1871.

On 7 August 1871, HRH the Duke of Edinburgh presented new Colours to the 99th Foot in the Guards enclosure at Aldershot. In his address he said, 'I do not think you will guard them [the Colours] less carefully because it is a sailor who has handed them to your safe keeping'. The officers receiving the Colours were Ens. Cooch (Queen's Colour) and Ens. Macklin (Regimental Colour). Although this photograph is not very clear, it is the earliest the museum has of a presentation of Colours to one of the battalions.

The old colours of the 99th Foot were presented to the Duke and Duchess of Edinburgh by Lt-Col. John Hart Dunne and his officers in September 1874. The Queen's Guard at Balmoral, provided by a company of the 99th, were drawn up at Ballanter railway station with the Colours. The Colours hung on the grand staircase of Clarence House in London until the Duke's death in 1900 and the following year were laid up in St James' church, Devizes. The officers on parade in this photograph were Lt-Col. Dunne, Capt. Wayman, Lt Macklin and Lt Weare.

This stand of Colours of the 99th Foot was the last to be carried in action, in the Zulu War in South Africa, 1879. During the Boer War they were kept at the Regimental Depot at Devizes. In 1926 they were brought back to England from India and laid up in Salisbury Cathedral where their remains can still be seen. An instruction of 1898 stated that when Colours were replaced they became the property of the state and had to be deposited in a church or other public building, instead of being at the disposal of the Colonel of the Regiment. This order was later reiterated with the statement 'in no circumstances may Colours be allowed to pass into the possession of any individual'. Although this instruction keeps these regimental treasures out of private hands, many just rot and turn to dust. It has become the practice with modern sets of Colours to enclose them in air-tight display cases and thereby increase their life span.

The 1st Battalion Colours, c.1884, South Camp Aldershot. Standing, left to right: Sgt Kane (master cook), Col-Sgt Osbourne, Sgt Dmr -?-, Col-Sgt -?- and Sgt Lewis. Sitting: Armourer Sgt Shenstone (with dog), Bdsm. Griffin, Paymaster Sgt -?-, Sgt-Maj. Burton, QM Sgt Ellis, Orderly Room Sgt Gabell and Ex-Sgt Humphries (who had fought with the 62nd Foot at at Ferozeshah in 1845). Front: Band Sgt Bartlett and Sgt Master Tailor Davis.

On their arrival at Aldershot, the battalion followed the old custom of 'crying down the credit'. For the best part of a day the drum-major paraded the streets with drums and fifes, signifying to the tradesmen of the town that they should not give credit to the men.

1st Battalion Guard of Honour in Quetta, c.1898, with the guard wearing khaki drill uniforms. After leaving Quetta the battalion went to Peshawar and Cherat. In 1905 they were still in India and it was said that the Queens and Wiltshires were the two best battalions in India. At this time the Wiltshires excelled in shooting and tug-of-war.

1st Battalion Guard of Honour in full ceremonial uniform at Quetta, India in 1899 during the visit of the Commander-in-Chief. The previous year on 14 January 1898, at Karachi, the battalion provided a Guard of Honour of three officers and 100 rank and file for the governor of Bombay at the opening of the Lady Dufferin Hospital. The King's Colour is carried in the centre with the band and drums located at the far end of the guard. This battalion remained in India during the Boer War but provided many soldiers to reinforce the 2nd Battalion in South Africa.

The warrant officers and sergeants of the 1st Battalion in Quetta, *c.*1899, together with their Colours. Maj. Steel is seated fourth from left in the second row. They had arrived at this station in 1898 after three unhealthy years in Karachi. At Quetta the battalion suffered fifty deaths from enteric fever. The attitude to killer diseases like enteric and cholera were summed up by Kipling:

> We've got the cholerer in camp – it's worse than forty fights;
> We're dyin' in the wilderness the same as Isrulites;
> It's before us, an' be'ind us, an' we cannot get away,
> An' the doctor's just reported we've ten more to-day!

A photograph of the regimental Colours of the French 99th Regiment d'Infanterie presented to the 2nd Battalion Wiltshire Regiment (formerly the 99th Foot) in 1913 when the battalion was stationed in Gibraltar. This French regiment was stationed at Lyon-Vienne when an attempt was made to forge links between the two regiments. The First World War that started the following year stopped any further collaboration and it was not revived after the war. The French Colour was adorned with the Légion d'honneur for the regiment's action at the Battle of Aculcingo, Mexico, in 1862. This photograph was presented to the officers of the 2nd Battalion. The French also presented the battalion with a set of clarions, which are still in the regimental museum.

The Colours and drums of the 2nd Battalion, Aldershot, in 1899, just prior to the Boer War. Left to right: Pte Rogers; Sgt Hart; Bdsm. Robins; Dmr Sutton; L/Cpl Bradley; L/Cpl Goodchild; 2nd-Lt Henslow. 2nd-Lt Henslow joined the battalion in 1897, serving in the Boer War and receiving a mention in Lord Kitchener's dispatches. On the outbreak of the First World War, he went to France with the battalion in command of D Company. On the evening of 23 October 1914 the CO of the 2nd Wilts was worried about the weakness of the left flank and sent Capt. Henslow to Brigade HQ to explain the situation. The next day the battalion was overwhelmed by a massive German assault and Capt. Henslow was among about 450 of the 2nd Battalion who were captured. He survived the war and was later promoted to major and awarded the Military Cross.

The escort and Colours of the 1st Battalion, Jhansi, India in 1909. This is where the battalion spent the last two years of its Indian service before going to South Africa. Jhansi in the Central Provinces was described as a railway station in the middle of a desert; although very hot it provided good game shooting. At this time, great emphasis was placed on drill and turnout. On 31 October 1909, the battalion embarked at Bombay on the *Dufferin* and sailed for South Africa on 1 November. The ship stopped enroute at the Seychelles on 7 November. During the voyage two deaths were recorded, one a lance corporal and the other a child.

The Colours of the 1st Battalion in South Africa, c.1910. They are being held by the drum major. The battalion arrived in Pietermaritzburg in 1909 having spent fourteen years in India. On 6 May 1910 approval was received for the Battle Honour Louisburg to be added to the colours – this was the regiment's first Battle Honour, won in 1758 in Canada. The battalion remained in South Africa until 1913. The Colours seen here were presented by Lt-Gen. W.T. Knollys at Aldershot on 18 May 1865, after which they were carried for seventy-four years, but never in action. They were laid up in St James' church, Devizes, in 1946.

The 2nd Battalion in full ceremonial dress at a parade in Dublin. This is believed to be the St Patrick's Day parade that took place on 17 March 1911. The battalion had arrived in Dublin in 1908 and remained there until 1912. On 19 August 1911 several companies of the battalion went to Llandudno Junction and Mold in Wales on strike breaking duties. After remaining for a short period providing guards (mostly at railway junctions) they returned to Dublin.

The presentation of new Colours to the 3rd Militia Battalion at Le Marchant Barracks, Devizes, 15 July 1913. The Colours were presented by Field Marshal Lord Methuen. This was the first set of militia Colours to bear the Battle Honours of the regular battalions. The old militia Colours, which had been presented in 1853, are seen here being marched past for the final time before they were laid up in St James' church, Devizes. Today they are held in the regimental museum in Salisbury.

The old and the new Colours of the 3rd Militia Battalion, 15 July 1913. Standing, left to right: Lts Stewart, Upton and Belcher, 2nd-Lt Goddard, Lt Watkin, 2nd-Lt Blyth, Capts Dyer and Martin, Lt Spencer, Capt. Magor, 2nd-Lts Cruikshank, Hockney and Barclay. Sitting: Capts Makin, Malet and Ceillard, Maj. Brown, Field Marshal Lord Methuen, Col. Barclay, Maj. Spiller, Capts Gillson, Reynolds and Cary-Barnard.

Capt. Dyer, DSO, was an ex-officer of the Life Guards who was on the special reserve of officers for the Wiltshire Militia. He was awarded the DSO for services in the Kano-Sokoto expedition in West Africa in 1902 and was the prospective parliamentary Liberal candidate for Salisbury in 1912. He died in 1917 and was buried in Madrid.

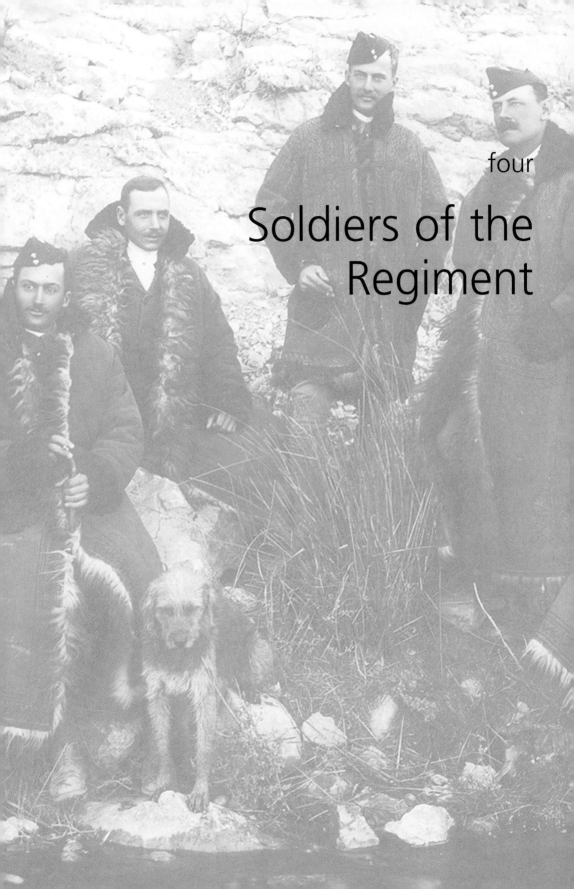

four

Soldiers of the Regiment

Above left: Lt-Col. James Johnson, the second CO of the 99th Foot, pictured here later in life. He was born in 1788 and his early military service was in the 40th Foot. He fought with that regiment in Montevideo, Uruguay, in 1807, and later in the Peninsula War at Vimiera and Talavera. He was later seconded to the Portuguese Army, eventually ending up as a lieutenant colonel commanding a brigade. On his return to England in 1825 he became a major in the 99th Foot and obtained command of the regiment in Mauritius at the age of forty. He later relinquished command in Ireland and retired in 1839. He handed command of the regiment to Lt-Col. Sir John Gaspard Le Marchant.

Above right: Lt-Col. Sir John Gaspard Le Marchant. Born in 1804, the son of a noted Peninsula general who was killed at Salamanca in 1812, he joined the 99th Foot in 1839 having purchased the lieutenant-colonelcy. Aged thirty-six when he took command, he was in effect junior to his majors, several of the captains and one of the subalterns. Known unofficially as 'Don Gaspard', he was a colourful character, who achieved great prestige for himself and his regiment. He stood no nonsense from his own officers and men, but even less from outsiders who tried to interfere with them. The Duke of Cambridge said later that the 99th Foot under Sir John were about the smartest and best-drilled regiment in the service. When the regiment embarked for Australia in 1842 Sir John exchanged once again and, in 1856, became a major-general. He was later the Governor of Newfoundland, Nova Scotia and Malta. In 1865 he received a KCB and commanded the Madras Army for three years. He died in 1874, aged seventy. Although his time in the 99th was short, his influence was such that the Regimental Depot in Devizes was named after him.

Above left: Maj.-Gen. John Napper Jackson. He was the first officer to serve in the 99th and subsequently become its Colonel. His army career started in the 94th Foot in 1805 at the age of nine and he was only fourteen when he commenced five years of active service in the Peninsula and was present at some thirty battles and actions including the storming of Ciudad Rodrigo, Nive, and Nivelle. He received the Peninsula Medal and ten clasps before he was nineteen. He joined the Light Company of the 99th on its formation in 1824 as an experienced fighting soldier with twenty year's service, but still only twenty-nine years old. He went with the regiment to Mauritius and Australia, where he acted in command for two years during Col. Despard's absence in New Zealand. He later commanded the regiment in Ireland and Aldershot where they gained a tremendous reputation for smartness in dress and drill. Afterwards described by a fellow officer as 'Moltke of the Nines' he was seldom seen off the barrack square and never known to go on leave. There was a regimental legend that he had once been observed in plain clothes! He became the Colonel of the Regiment from 1863 until his death at the age of seventy in 1866.

Above right: Lt-Col. George Marmaduke Reeves, CB, 99th Foot. He joined the army in 1825 and entered the 99th as a captain four years later. He commanded the Grenadier Company and was initially described by his follow officers as being high-minded. He went with his regiment to Australia in 1842 and later took the regiment to India in 1854, the year he took command. In 1860 he sailed with the 99th for the war in China and was given command of a brigade on arrival, handing over command of the regiment to Lt-Col. Henry James Day. On the way to Pekin, he achieved his ambition of being under fire before he died. He was made a CB for his services during that campaign. Promoted to major-general in 1865, he died the following year, aged sixty-five.

Maj. George Jean de Winton joined the 99th Foot in 1841 and was stationed in Chatham and Sheerness until 1843 when he was placed in command of the military guard on the convict ship *Constant*, bound for Van Diemen's Land. The governor of that colony at the time was Sir John Franklin, fated to perish in the frozen wastes of the Arctic. The Major and Sir John became steadfast friends. Maj. de Winton remained in the antipodes until 1853, doing military duty at Norfolk Island, Sydney, Brisbane, Bathhurst and various other places. During this period he saw service several times against the aborigines. The town of Winton in Queensland was named after him, and one of the principal streets in Brisbane also bears his name. He again saw active service during the Crimean War, where he was the brigade major of the Anglo-Swiss legion. He was for some time the editor of the *United Service Magazine* and produced a book entitled *Soldiering Fifty Years Ago. Australia in the Forties*. He was a regular contributor to the regimental magazine *The Nines*, writing under the pseudonym 'Chateau'. He died in 1898. (There is doubt over the naming of the town, Winton, although recently the local council requested copies of photographs of Maj. Winton for the town hall.)

Sgt Thomas Johnson, 99th Foot, pictured here in 1872 when he retired after twenty-one years' service. He enlisted in in Dublin in 1848 at the age of fifteen, serving with the regiment in Australia, India, China, Cape of Good Hope and England. In 1926, when addressing the Old Comrades Association, he described his journey to Van Diemen's Land when he acted as one of the guards of 400 prisoners taken on-board at Kingstown, Ireland. It took them five months to reach Tasmania. The prisoners of whom he had charge were those taken in connection with the Fenian uprisings of 1849–50. His progression through the ranks was steady, apart from one incident which resulted in him being reduced from sergeant to private in 1865. Four years later he regained his previous rank, which he retained until he retired. On being discharged he was immediately admitted as an out-pensioner at the Royal Hospital at Chelsea. After leaving the army, he turned his hand to music and taught the violin and piano. He died in 1928.

Cpl George Bryant, 62nd Foot, was born in Kensington, London, in 1843. He lived in Bradford-on-Avon, Wiltshire, enlisting into the regiment in 1860. Joining the battalion in Nova Scotia he later served in Ireland (1866–68) and India, at Lucknow and Barrackpore. While in India he won two Queen's Army Best Shot Medals, for 1871 and 1872 which he is seen wearing in this photograph. He was presented with the Silver Medal in 1871 in a general parade before the entire brigade by Maj.-Gen. Sir Henry Tombs, KCB, VC, commanding the Oudh Division. He was ill for a number of years and died in India at the age of thirty-five. The Army Best Shot Medal, authorised in 1869, became obsolete in 1883, but was reinstated in 1923, as the King's Medal for the Champion Shot in the Army. The 62nd Foot also furnished the champion shot for the British Army in 1866 (Cpl C. Smith) and 1869–70 (Sgt C. Rogers).

Gen. Sir John Hart Dunne, KCB, was the first official Colonel of the amalgamated 62nd and 99th Foot. He initially joined the 62nd, but most of his service was with the 99th. He fought in the Crimean War with the 21st Foot (Royal Scots Fusiliers), after which he exchanged into the 99th Foot, remaining with them for twenty-one years, more than half of which was as CO. In 1860 he went to China on active service with his regiment. Whilst there he was attached to the staff for a short period and personally hoisted the Union Jack over the captured Taku Forts. In 1865 he took command of the 99th Foot, remaining in command until 1877. In 1881 he was promoted to major-general, becoming a general in 1893. At this time he became Lieutenant of the Tower of London, a position he held until 1897. He became the Colonel of the Regiment in 1898 remaining so until 1924 when he died at the age of eighty-nine. His son followed him into the regiment for a short time, but left to become a well-known aeroplane designer between the world wars.

Above left: Lt-Col. Henry James Day, 99th Foot, joined the regiment as an ensign in 1825, becoming the adjutant three years later. His postings included Mauritius and the Maori Wars in New Zealand. He commanded the regiment during the China War of 1860 and in all served in the regiment for thirty-nine years. He married the daughter of the paymaster of the 99th in 1832, with his second son (also named Henry James) following him into the regiment. His third child, Catherine, retained her link with the regiment when she married Capt. D.J. Molson of the 99th.

Above right: Lt-Col. Henry James Day, 99th Foot, son of the above, joined the regiment in 1854 at the age of nineteen, and became the adjutant in 1860. Thus, during the China War the 99th had a father and son team at its head. Henry James II reached the rank of major, retiring in 1864 with the honorary rank of lieutenant colonel. After retirement he commuted his pension, invested it badly and lost heavily. Consequently, his second son, A.F. Day, left Lancing School and enlisted into the 62nd Foot, later transferring to the Dorsetshire Regiment. His fourth son, F.I. Day, was killed in action whilst commanding the Royal Munster Fusiliers in December 1914 at Givenchy. In 1926 his grandson F. Day also joined the Wiltshire Regiment, retiring in 1951 as a lieutenant colonel. Henry James Day died in 1892.

Above left: Lt-Col. William Lennox Ingall, CB, joined the 62nd Foot at Dinapore in India in 1843. In 1844 the regiment was ordered to Umballa and en route were diverted to Ferozepore because of the possible hostilities with the Sikh nation. This entailed a journey by road and river of a thousand miles; during this trek, Ingall carried the regimental Colour for the complete journey. He was wounded by grapeshot on the first day of the Battle of Ferozeshah, 21 December 1845, but remained at his post and fought the following day. Later he commanded a company at Sobraon. He went with the regiment to the Crimea where in June 1855 part of his thigh was carried away by the round shot that killed the Commanding Officer, Lt-Col. Shearman, and killed or wounded eighteen of the 62nd's rank and file. In October, a second CO was killed, giving Maj. Ingall his lieutenant-colonelcy and command of the regiment. He was invalided home but returned to the Crimea as soon as he could. In 1856 he took command of the regiment in Canada, where this picture was taken, commanding it for the next fourteen years in Nova Scotia, Aldershot, Ireland and India. In 1870 he was promoted to brigadier general in Bengal, and in 1873 a major general in command of the Allahabad Division. He retired in 1882 and died in 1888.

Above right: Maj. Henry Charles Harford was born in Bangalore in 1852. He went to Africa in 1864 where he settled down on the family estate, Stapleton Grove, at Pinetown, near Durban. Returning to England in 1870, he was accepted as an ensign in the 99th Foot. On the outbreak of the Zulu War he applied for special service because of his knowledge of the country and his ability to speak the Zulu language. On arrival in South Africa he was assigned to the 3rd Natal Native Contingent (NNC). His unit was part of the centre column (which included the 24th Foot) during the invasion of Zululand. He camped at Isandlwana but left to scout the outlying area. This order saved his life, as the camp was later overwhelmed and the 24th Regiment almost wiped out. He was later present at the Mzinyathi River near Fugitives' Drift when the Colours of the 24th Foot were recovered and was given the honour of carrying these Colours back to the camp of the remnants of the 24th. After the 3rd NNC was disbanded, he returned to the 99th and went with the regiment to Bermuda before coming back to South Africa in 1881. He took command of the 2nd Battalion in 1898. Keenly interested in natural history, many specimens from his collection can be found in the museum at Durban. He was a also very good artist and his drawings of incidents in the Zulu War were published in the *Illustrated London News* of 1879, attracting considerable attention. He died in 1937.

Pte Joseph Bathe, the last known survivor of the 99th Foot who fought in the Zulu War. Joining the regiment in 1878; he left England for South Africa in December that year. He claimed that during one of the battles against the Zulus he was wounded in the foot by a poisoned Zulu spear but a comrade sucked out the poison and saved his life. He later remembered that the hardest time in Natal was when he took part in a thirty-two mile forced march, fighting and digging trenches against the Zulus whose estimated casualties on this day were 2,000 at Gingindlovu. After this campaign he went to Bermuda where he was presented with his campaign medal. He returned to South Africa with the 99th Foot in 1881 for the First Boer War, but hostilities ceased before they arrived. In Cape Town he was transferred to the band where he played the bassoon and clarinet. In 1887 he was part of the massed bands at Peshawar for Queen Victoria's Golden Jubilee. Later in life he became a firm supporter of the Regimental Association, attending many reunions. He died in 1953.

Col-Sgt A. Osborne enlisted into the regiment at Devizes in 1878. His potential was quickly recognised and he was promoted to lance-corporal on completion of his training. He was posted to the 99th Foot, (later the 2nd Battalion) serving two tours in India. Subsequently he became an instructor to F and G Companies of the 2nd Volunteer Battalion at Swindon. He is seen here in the uniform of the Volunteers. He retired in 1908, with the rank of colour sergeant with thirty years service to his credit. On leaving the Army he obtained employment as the chief clerk with the Wiltshire Territorial Association. He was very good at gymnastics, a first-class fencing instructor and had the reputation of being one of the finest exponents of old-time dancing in the county. He was the holder of the Meritorious Service Medal and died in Swindon in 1939.

Sgt Henry Robert Stimson, 99th Foot, was born in Ely, Cambridgeshire. He enlisted into the regiment in 1856, giving his age as eighteen, when in fact he was fifteen, and served for twenty-one years and eleven months, completing his engagement in 1878. He served with the 99th during the China War of 1860. This photograph was taken in 1865 on the occasion of his promotion to the rank of sergeant. Prior to this he had one demotion in 1864 from corporal to private for 'quitting the barracks when on gate duty'. He quickly regained his rank and retired as a sergeant major. On retirement he joined the 3rd East Surrey Militia, serving for six years. His wife Rosanna came from Dublin. They had six children – one of whom (Henry) joined the Wiltshire Regiment and another the Royal Artillery. During the First World War he served in the Scottish Company of the City of London National Guard, he was aged seventy-four and still wearing uniform. He died in 1923. This photograph is of interest as it shows his pillbox-style headdress lacks the diced band which was introduced for the 99th in 1867.

Col-Sgt Henry Stimson, DCM, 2nd Battalion – son of the above – pictured here in 1906 when the battalion was stationed in Pembroke Dock in Wales. He enlisted in 1890 into the Argyll and Sutherland Highlanders at the age of eighteen, giving his occupation as a tea sampler. In 1895 he transferred into the 2nd Battalion, the Wiltshire Regiment, as a corporal and in doing so joined his father's old regiment. In 1897 he was appointed as the battalion Provost Sergeant. He served with the battalion during the Boer War. He took part in many actions and was awarded the DCM in the battalion's action at Slabbert's Nek on 23 July 1900. There he came close to death when a Boer bullet smashed his rifle butt. He was also Mentioned in Dispatches. Although he survived the Boer War unhurt he became, in effect, a late casualty of the conflict, as he contracted tuberculosis brought about by exposure in South Africa and in 1906 his health began to fail. On 5 June that year he reverted to sergeant at his own request and nine months later he was discharged as medically unfit. Stimson died in 1908 aged just thirty-six.

Above left: Maj. Arthur Alison Stuart Barnes was born on 9 July 1867 in Kashmir, India. He was a cadet at the Royal Military College in 1885–86, became a lieutenant in the 2nd Battalion on 25 August 1886 and subsequently served in India and Burma until 1895. He was the first editor of the regimental magazine, *The Nines,* which he managed for a number of years. He received his captaincy on 15 January 1895, and was appointed adjutant of the battalion. Three years later he was selected to go to Wei-Hai-Wei, China, to assist in the formation of the Chinese Regiment. He took part in the Relief of Tientsin in the China War of 1900 and commanded the detachment of the 1st Chinese Regiment on the march to, and subsequent relief of, Pekin in August 1900. Mentioned in Dispatches on 14 May 1901, he also received the China Medal with the clasp, 'Relief of Peking'. Maj. Barnes wrote a book detailing his service in China entitled *On Active Service with the Chinese Regiment.* He returned to the Wiltshire Regiment after the Boer War, leaving around 1908. He served in the First World War but not in any of the Wiltshire battalions. Maj. Barnes died on 3 May 1937 at Worthing, Sussex, England. The photograph shows him as a lieutenant around 1886. Note that the white collar facings of his mess dress tunic clearly show the badges of the Wiltshire Regiment.

Above right: Lt Francis Dansey. He was commissioned in 1898, joining the 2nd Battalion in Quetta, where we see him in this photograph. He was the adjutant from 1909 to 1912 followed by a period on the staff. On the outbreak of the First World War he was deputy assistant adjutant and quartermaster general of the North Midland Division, Territorial Force. During the war he was Mentioned in Dispatches four times and was awarded the Distinguished Service Order in 1916. He commanded the 1st Battalion from 1923–27 in Tidworth, where the battalion excelled themselves at the searchlight tattoos and later at Plymouth. He was a good all-round sportsman, hunter, and cricketer, he went on to command the 2nd Battalion just prior to his retirement in 1932. He died in 1953.

Maj. Thomas Edward Verner, 62nd Foot, exchanged into the regiment after serving in the 37th Foot (Hampshire Regiment). He had previously served in Bengal as an officer on famine relief operations and in Afghanistan as a transport officer to Sir W. Stewart during the campaign of 1878–80. He served with the 62nd Foot in the East Indies and Aden. Fluent in both French and Hindustani, he is shown here dressed in the style adopted by officers of the regiment on the North West Frontier. In 1883 he exchanged once more into the Lincolnshire Regiment. The regular exchange between regiments was not unusual, as officers attempted to gain experience and thus increase their chances of promotion. At that time, if they stayed in one regiment any further advancement was very much a question of stepping into dead man's shoes.

A group of 1st Battalion officers at Charua Taugi Camp, Quetta, India, in December 1899. Left to right: Lts Monreal, T. Parker and Timmis, Maj. L Steel and Lt R. Majoribanks. George Monreal had previously been in the 2nd Battalion in Alderney where he was the temporary editor of the *The Nines*. In 1918 he became the CO of the 6th (Service) Battalion and was killed in action on 10 April 1918.

Alexander Timmis joined the battalion in 1898 and was a very fine horseman and polo player. On the outbreak of the First World War he was in command of A Company, 1st Battalion, where he performed with distinction at the first Battle of Ypres and was awarded the Military Cross. Taken prisoner at the same time, he spent the remainder of the war in captivity. He later commanded the 2nd Battalion in Bangalore in 1924, retiring in 1927.

Above left: Capt. Walter Sidney Brown, 2nd Battalion, pictured here shortly after the Boer War, wearing his South African War campaign medals. He was born in 1871 and educated at Harrow. Prior to joining the regiment he served in the 7th (Militia) King's Royal Rifle Corps. During the Boer War he was wounded at Rensburg on 12 February 1900 and Mentioned in Dispatches. Whilst in South Africa he sat as a board member, together with Lt Matcham, on the court martial of Lt 'Breaker' Morant – an officer of the Bushveldt Carbineers – who stood accused, with other officers of that unit, of murdering Boer prisoners. Lt Morant was found guilty and sentenced to death, with a plea for clemency from the board. This was rejected and Morant was executed. A film starring Edward Woodward was later made about this incident. After the Boer War, Brown served as a staff captain in the Wessex (Territorial) Division. During the First World War he took command of the 2nd Battalion after the battle of Neuve Chapelle, remaining with them until June when he went to the 1st Battalion. He commanded the 1st Battalion between 1 July 1915 until he was killed in action at Thiepval on 4 July 1916. He was the longest serving Wiltshire battalion commander on the Western Front. He was buried in Blighty Valley Cemetery, Authuile Wood.

Above right: Capt. Edward Evans, DSO, 2nd Battalion, seen here after the Boer War in full dress uniform, wearing his Distinguished Service Order (DSO) and Boer War campaign medals. He joined the regiment in 1893 and served in the 2nd Battalion as adjutant in the Boer War winning the DSO for rescuing a wounded soldier under fire. He himself was later seriously wounded when, during a night attack, he fell over a 60ft cliff narrowly escaping with his life. After this incident he remained in South Africa becoming the Garrison Adjutant at Pietermaritzburg. During the First World War he served most of his time in the Middle East and was Mentioned in Dispatches five times. In 1918 he was appointed ADC to the King and was created a CMG in 1918 and a CB in 1919. After the war he became a staff captain in the Home Counties Division, Eastern Command, carrying out a number of other staff appointments before retiring in 1934 as a major-general. On retirement he became the Colonel of the Regiment, an appointment he held until 1942. He died in 1949 aged seventy-seven.

Above left: Sgt James Light, another regimental crack shot. He was born at Seend, near Devizes, in 1862, enlisting into the regiment in 1883 and serving in the 2nd Battalion in India, Burma and South Africa (Boer War). He was promoted to sergeant in 1888 and colour sergeant in 1898. After the Boer War he was posted to the Salisbury detachment of the 1st Wilts Volunteer Corps, serving with them for nine years before retiring in 1910. In 1915 after the outbreak of war he rejoined, acting as a drill instructor throughout Wiltshire in helping to train the war-raised units. He was then promoted to Regimental Quartermaster Sergeant with the 5th (Volunteer) Somerset Light Infantry. At the end of the war he again retired with thirty-two years' service to his credit. His shooting record was:

1888	Silver shield for the best shot in the NCOs' team at Meerut, India.
1889	Silver cup presented by Sir Ian Hamilton at the Meerut Central Rifle Meeting, also the silver shield as a member of the successful inter-regiment team.
1890	Silver shield in the 'Honour and Glory' match for all India, which was won by the Wiltshire Regiment.
1892	Bronze medal at the army versus volunteers rifle meeting.
1893	Silver medal presented by the Maharajah of Hyderabad for shooting at 800, 900 and 1,000 yards. The competition was fired with the old Martini rifle, that being the last year it was issued.
1893	Bronze medal, third in the championship of all India.
1894	Silver medal and championship of Burma.
1914	Donegal badge at Devizes Miniature Rifle meeting.

Above right: Pte (later Sgt) Joseph Bridewell, 2nd Battalion, pictured here in his dress uniform wearing his Queen's and King's Medals for service in the Boer War. He was the eldest of eight children, his parents being farmers at Five Lanes Farm, Whistley, Potterne, near Devizes. He ran away to join the army, lying about his age. His family bought him out of the army twice but he returned and eventually remained. With his brother Herbert, he served in the 1st Battalion in the First World War. They were together on 3 May 1916 when a German mine exploded under the company bombers' position. Herbert died in his brother's arms. Joseph survived the war, after which he took up employment at Pewsey Mental Hospital.

Above left: Rifleman William Smith (seated), 1st Battalion Wiltshire Volunteer Rifle Corps. He enlisted in 1885 and two years later was chosen as one of the four volunteers to be present at the laying of the Trowbridge Town Hall foundation stone. The same year, 1887, he took part in the review at Aldershot to commemorate the Golden Jubilee of Queen Victoria. Ten years later he was in the Guard of Honour in London for the Diamond Jubilee. For twenty years he was the armourer at the Drill Hall in St Thomas's Passage, Trowbridge and, was one of the founding members of the Trowbridge Voluntary Fire Brigade. During the First World War he served in both the Wiltshire Regiment and Somerset Light Infantry on the east coast. He died in 1953 aged eighty-four. He is seen here wearing the uniform of the Wiltshire Volunteers which were based on Rifle green and black, together with the busby, reflecting the Rifle Brigade uniform. The 1st Volunteer Battalion badge at this time was a black bugle.

Above right: Mr William Stancomb, of Blount's Court, Potterne, pictured here in the uniform of the Wiltshire Militia, *c.*1870. He was a lieutenant in the militia and at the time this photograph was taken he was attached to the Scots Guards for training. Born in 1850 at Trowbridge, he married Frances Milward in 1873. They had five children. For many years he was a Justice of the Peace in Marden, East Coulston and Devizes. In 1928 he remembered the militia of old as:

> Shepherd lads from the downs, and stout ruddy-cheeked chawbacons from the north, with the clay still hanging about their iron-shod lace-ups, some of whom have trudged their thirty miles with nought of victual to support the inner man but raw carrots – a bad stratum for Devizes beer, which has fermented accordingly, and produced the state called muzzy. Here and there a collier lad from the western border shows, ragged and grimy, and a pothouse help or adventurous stable-boy, in dilapidated corduroys, and a bit of hay in hapless decadence … chewing straws, and sporting a top-sawyer air of devil-may-care.

He died in 1941, aged ninety-one and was buried at St Mary the Virgin, Potterne, Wiltshire.

Above left: Lt-Col. Henry Molyneux Carter was born in 1850 and joined the 62nd Foot in 1868. In 1878 he served in the Khyber Pass during the Afghan War, afterwards being on the staff in Bengal. He commanded the 2nd Battalion during the Boer War where he was slightly wounded at Slabbert's Nek. Later he was more seriously wounded at Slap Krantz, receiving a CB for his actions. During his command in South Africa two rifle companies were captured by the Boers at Rensburg due to a break down of communication during a night-time withdrawal operation. Lt-Col. Carter accepted full responsibility for this but was exonerated by the board of enquiry. It was pointed out that the night of this action was his sixteenth night without sleep and no blame could be attached. After relinquishing command he was made a brevet colonel and served as Chief Inspector of Army Ordnance Depots until retiring in 1907. He had a great love for the regiment and was the regimental historian of his time, writing under the initials H.M.C. His records are still in use to this day. His son also joined the regiment. Lt-Col. Carter died in 1914.

Above right: Capt. Carleton Hooper Morrison Kirkwood, pictured here in 1888. He was educated at Cheltenham and was gazetted into the 2nd West India Regiment in 1882. In 1884 he became the Garrison Adjutant, Jamaica. He exchanged into the Wiltshire Regiment in 1888 and was promoted to major in 1900. The same year he went to South Africa, where he joined the 2nd Battalion on 3 March. He initially became the commandant of the towns of Waterval north, and later Pietpotgietersrust. He commanded the 2nd Battalion from 20 July 1900 to 9 February 1901, taking part in the battalion actions at Bethlehem, and Wittebergen after Col. Carter was wounded. He was Mentioned in Dispatches and later received the DSO from the King for his services in South Africa. From 1906 to 1909 he commanded the 1st Battalion in India and retired with the rank of colonel in 1910. Recalled on the outbreak of the First World War in 1914 he went to France where he was employed on lines of communication. He was twice Mentioned in Dispatches and was awarded a CMG in 1918. He died in 1937 at the age of seventy-seven.

Officers of the 1st Battalion who formed part of the 2nd Mounted Infantry at Harrismith, South Africa, 1910. Left to right: Lts Kirwin and de Crespigny, Capt. Timmis, Lts Davis and Seagrave. Lt Seagrave joined the battalion in 1908 and was later seconded to the West African Frontier Force until 1915. During the First World War he went to France on the staff, then joined the Royal Flying Corps. After the war he returned to the 2nd Battalion, of which he took command in 1935. He died in 1956.

Lt Claude Vierville Champion de Crespigny came from a long line of military officers in Essex. He enlisted as a private in the Imperial Yeomanry in 1900, later joining the Wiltshire Regiment where he was commissioned. In 1905/06 he was seconded to the King's African Rifles. He left the regiment in 1910, joining the 3rd (Militia) Essex Regiment. On the outbreak of the First World War he joined the 2nd Battalion Suffolk Regiment, surviving the war and retiring as a major. After the war he became a game ranger in Tanganyika, where he died in 1927.

Lt-Col. L.H. Warden (left) pictured here together with the QM Capt. Cordon en route to England from South Africa in 1913 on HMT *Rohilla*. Louis Warden was born in 1862 and joined the regiment in 1881. From 1889 to 1894 he was attached to the Army Service Corps. Serving as the adjutant of the 3rd Battalion from 1897 to 1902, he commanded them on St Helena during the Boer War. He was CO of the 1st Battalion from January 1910 to April 1913. He died from jaundice on 24 January 1914 aged fifty-one. Capt. Cordon, an old soldier of the regiment, was given a quartermaster's commission in 1908, and was the quartermaster of the 1st Battalion on the outbreak of the First World War. He was largely responsible for the smooth mobilisation of the battalion. During the war he was Mentioned in Dispatches twice.

Above left: Cpl Frederick Hobson joined the 1st Battalion at Athlone in 1887. Appointed as a drummer in 1889, he remained with the battalion until 1898 when he was posted to the 2nd Battalion, with which he fought in the Boer War. He served in F Company and was mentioned in Earl Roberts' dispatches, 10 September 1901, for special and meritorious service. After the war he served at the regimental depot and was then discharged in 1902 after fifteen years' service. He then emigrated to Canada. He was married and had several children. On the outbreak of the First World War he attempted to re-enlist but was refused by the doctors. Undaunted by this rejection he went to a different town where he enlisted into the 20th Battalion, Canadian Expeditionary Force at Toronto. It was with that battalion that he went to the Western Front in France. There on 18 August 1917 at Hill 70, during a strong enemy attack he took over a Lewis gun after the crew had been killed. The weapon jammed and he rushed the advancing enemy with bayonet and rifle butt until he himself was shot dead. For this action he was awarded the Victoria Cross. He has no known grave and is commemorated on the Vimy Memorial to the missing.

Above right: Capt. Frederick William Stoddart, 1st Battalion. Born in 1871 he served for five years in the ranks of the Royal Inniskilling Fusiliers. He received his commission in the Wiltshire Regiment in 1895, becoming a lieutenant in 1897 and spending several years in India with the 1st Battalion. He served for five years from January 1900 to January 1905 in the Chinese Regiment at Wei-Hai-Wei and took part in the relief of Pekin in 1900 for which he received the medal with clasp. From September 1908 to October 1912 he was adjutant of the 4th (Territorial) Battalion Welsh Regiment. Subsequently he returned to the Wiltshire Regiment, serving with the 2nd Battalion at Pembroke Dock and the 1st Battalion at Tidworth.

On the outbreak of the First World War he went to France with the 1st Battalion which formed part of the 7th Infantry Brigade. Leaving England on 13 August 1914 for the front, Capt. Stoddart was soon awarded the Légion d'honneur for special gallantry during the operations between 21 and 30 August. On 27 October 1914 he was killed at Neuve Chapelle. Capt. Stoddart's company became surrounded but he would not surrender. Lt-Col. Oliphant, who was taken prisoner in the same action, later said, 'Captain Stoddart was last seen standing on the parapet of his trench firing at the advancing Germans – a very brave and lone suicidal figure.' He has no known grave and is commemorated on the Le Touret Memorial, Pas de Calais, France.

Sgt Tom King, 1st Battalion, together with his wife Sarah and daughter Mabel outside their married quarters in Tidworth, just prior to his discharge in 1913. He enlisted in 1892 giving a false name of George King. He served in both battalions in India and South Africa, including the Boer War. He later wrote an account of his time during the Boer War, which was serialised in the regimental journal. Standing behind him are his two brothers Arthur and Henry, also serving in the battalion. Sgt King's discharge documents state, 'recommended for employment in any place of trust, would prefer employment as postman'. He retired to Bath Road, Swindon.

Lt Walter Richard Augustus Aston Dawes was born in Salisbury in 1878, the son of Mr Frederick Dawes, the official receiver of the city. In 1896 he joined the 1st Wiltshire Rifle Volunteers as a private, being appointed as a Second Lieutenant three years later. He resigned the position in 1900, enlisted into the Volunteer Service Company of the Wiltshire Regiment and proceeded to South Africa to serve in the Boer War. Whilst there he was promoted through the ranks, serving at one time with the mounted infantry as a sergeant major. On returning to England he gained a commission in the regular battalion, subsequently serving in India between 1901 and 1909. From 1906 to 1908 he was the Cantonment Magistrate at Dagshai, and for part of that time was in charge of Dagshai Military Prison, which included some men from his own battalion as inmates. In 1909 he went to the regimental depot at Devizes, remaining until 1911 when he was promoted to captain and posted to the 1st Battalion, joining them in Natal. On the outbreak of the First World War he went to France with the 1st Battalion and on 23 August 1914 he was killed in action. He was the first officer of the 1st Battalion to lose his life in the First World War. He has no known grave and is commemorated as missing at Nouvelles Communal Cemetery.

five

Barrack Life

Le Marchant Barracks, Devizes, the regimental depot of the Wiltshire Regiment. Opened in 1878 it was named after Sir Gaspard Le Marchant, who had commanded the 99th Foot thirty-six years previously. It had accommodation for 250 men and became the focal point for administration for the volunteer and militia battalions within Wiltshire. This early photograph, believed to have been taken in the late 1890s, shows a recruit squad outside the main gate, a familiar sight for generations of Wiltshire Regiment recruits, whose first view of the depot would be the massive castellated keep.

A photograph taken from the top of the keep at Le Marchant Barracks, looking towards Devizes, taken just before the First World War. The onlookers are in their Sunday best as the troops march back to the barracks behind the band after a church parade at Southbroom church, Devizes. The fields to the right are now built-up areas.

An early photograph, *c.*1880, showing the barrack blocks inside Le Marchant Barracks. The grass area was later covered with tarmac. The barracks had its own married quarters, hospital and cricket ground. It was said that prior to the First World War, the Wiltshires were second only to the Suffolks in gaining recruits from within their respective counties, with the Suffolk Regiment claiming 99 per cent and the Wiltshires 98 per cent. All those recruits would have been housed in the barrack blocks seen here.

The officers' mess, Le Marchant Barracks, Devizes, just prior to the First World War. This was very much the officers' home and had the feel of a country club. The depot staff at this time included a major from the home battalion, a captain from the overseas battalion, a subaltern from each battalion to train the regular recruits and two captains to instruct the militia recruits. The officers changed every two years, returning to their respective battalions.

The band and drums, 2nd Battalion, India during 1882–83, having recently arrived there from South Africa. In order to avoid the summer heat, most of the battalion went to the hills. In this case the band and drums were part of the HQ group in the Kuldunnah district in the Murray Hills. Some are accompanied by their wives and children. Many of these men would have taken part in the Zulu War and some can be seen here wearing their campaign medals.

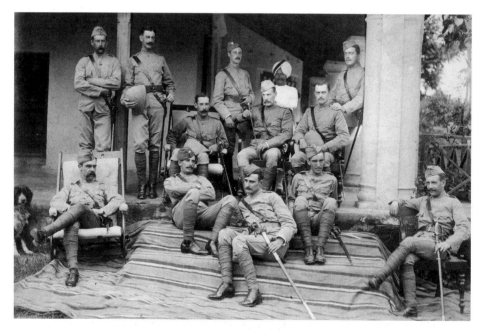

The officers, 1st Battalion, Subathu, India, 1888. Standing, left to right: Capts G. Hatch and A. Payne, Lts W. Rocke and E. Eicke. Centre, sitting: Lt A. Jeffreys, Lt-Col. C. Harvey and Lt R. Snow. Front, sitting: Maj. Russell, Lts R. Dill, H. Welman, A. Barnes and G. Dickson.

Lt-Col. Harvey was responsible for purchasing the printing press that later produced *The Nines*. The first editor was Lt A. Barnes. The battalion was the best shooting battalion in India for the years 1888, 1889 and 1890, and had the best shot in the British Army at that time, L/Cpl Viney, who in the presence of Lord Roberts in Simla in 1888 made 104 consecutive bullseyes at 900 yards standing.

The regimental crest of the 2nd Battalion at Cherat 1887, overlooking the parade and polo ground. Capt. Strachan oversaw the construction. The crest was drawn on white paper, then scaffolding was erected with a Jacob's Ladder leading up to it, the paper crest was pasted on, and Pte Newell, (one of the battalion pioneers) and his assistant carved it into the rock. It took several months to complete and it was finished off in white paint on black to make it stand out. It is about 6ft x 7ft in size and is still visible to this day.

A similar exercise was carried out by the 1st Battalion at Cherat, India in 1902. This time the work was carried out by L/Cpl Hindon. The 1st Battalion badge was not on such a grand scale as the 2nd Battalion, but nevertheless is still visible today. The regimental digest of service reads, 'On 15 Oct 1902, India, Cherat. Headquarters, A, B, C and G Companies leave for Peshawar and arrive there on 17 October. During stay at Cherat, Battalion Crest cut in rocks.'

Whilst the 1st Battalion were in Karachi in 1897 a plague took hold, killing many thousands of locals. Without good discipline the local British forces were as vulnerable as anyone else. The Wiltshire Regiment lost no soldiers to the plague. Here we see the Plague Detachment, under the command of Lt T. Roche. A Government instruction read:

> The treasury officer at Karachi is authorised to issue to the commanding officer 1st Wiltshire Regiment, the sum of rupees sixteen thousand three hundred and seventy three, annas two and pies one only, on account of plague duty pay. The amount is chargeable to the civil department, Bombay.

Soldiers of the examining guard from the 1st Battalion on segregated plague duty in Karachi, 1897. Their role was to set up road blocks to stop the local population travelling and also to conduct house to house searches to locate dead bodies and arrange for supervised disposal. The plague unit was also responsible, together with the civil authorities, for isolating incoming Indian Army units and passengers from ships. The battalion remained on this duty until the plague subsided.

Plague Duty Certificate.

Certified that No. 2890 Private S. Bodman 1st Battn Wiltshire Regiment was employed on Plague Duty in Karachi from 25th March 1897 till 7th August 1897 and that he did good work.

He was chiefly employed on Sanitary duty.

By order of His Excellency the Right Honourable the Governor in Council,

Bombay Castle,

(Date) 7th April 1899

Chief Secretary to Government.

No. 2135

A Plague Duty certificate issued to Pte 2390 A. Bodman, 1st Battalion, who was employed on plague duty at Karachi from 25 March to 7 August 1897, confirming that he did 'good' work. He was chiefly employed on sanitary duty. A detachment under Lt Beadon on duty at Sukkur later wrote:

> The detachment furnishes a patrol of three men nightly on the bridge – this duty being performed during the day by the native police; they prevent all intercourse between Sukkur and Rohri. Our chief duty consists in searching for the plague-stricken, finding them, and sending those affected off to hospital, whilst segregating other remainder.

The barrack room of F Company, 2nd Battalion, Fort Dufferin, Mandalay, July 1895. The battalion spent two years in Burma before returning to England in October the same year having been relieved by the Royal Scots. When they left Burma 500 men were cross posted to the 1st Battalion in India with the remaining 961 of all ranks returning to England.

The 2nd Battalion signallers, Mandalay, October 1895. Although the regiment was not deployed on active service, fifteen signallers from the battalion were attached to the Army Signalling Department and marched to join the Miranza Field Force in 1891, earning the India General Service Medal 1854–98 with clasp Samana. Two signallers from the detachment were commended, Ptes Charlton and Franklin. Although not named, several of these signallers are wearing their medal ribbons for that campaign. The frustrations of the signaller's task at this time were summed up in a poem in *The Nines* entitled 'A Kasauli', *Signallers Song*. The chorus went 'For its dash, dot, dash, all a'coming thick and fast, and every flash apparently exactly like the last, So don't lose your hair, if you can't read them right, you can read 'em at the other end by calling up for light'.

The 1st Battalion members of the Royal Army Temperance Association, Jhansi, India, in 1909. At this time, temperance societies were springing up all over Britain, a development mirrored within the army with the formation of the Army Temperance Society. Proven abstinence was rewarded with medals such as those which these members of the 1st Battalion are wearing. Both battalions had their fair share of drinkers and abstainers. Pte John Thatcher of the 2nd Battalion later remembered: 'We were the greatest "Drys" in India, and in 1887 The Nines headed the Gregson Army, later the Army Temperance Association, by 450 pledged abstainers and for the years 1890-1892 we were the best conducted Battalion in India, Long live The Nines and God save the King'.

The 1st Battalion branch of the Army Temperance Association held an evening of variety entertainment at Napier Barracks, Karachi, on 20 April 1897. The main part of the show was a comic sketch entitled *Touched, the Story of Doctor Mayburn's Asylum*. Cast were Pte Nalden, Pte Tiernan, Pte Cooper, Pte Elkins and Pte Short. Entertainment of this type was a regular occurrence, with some of the performances reaching a very high standard. It was not unknown for some drinkers to give up the drink temporarily in order to attend, only to lapse afterwards. Lt-Col. W.B. Williams, the CO, commanded the 1st Battalion for a short period in 1894, then the 2nd between 1894 and 1895, returning to the 1st Battalion again durng 1895 and 1898. After leaving the battalion he commanded the depot at Devizes.

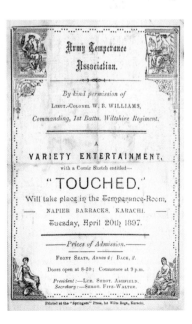

Drink was a major problem for the army at this time, as it was for society in general. The Army Temperance Society was the main organisation that helped soldiers to 'stay dry', but there were many others. Here in India, we see a group from the 1st Battalion of the Independent Order of Good Templars, a worldwide organisation dedicated to abstinence. This order was founded in Utica, New York in 1850 as the 'Knights of Jericho', a secret fraternal temperance society. They claimed that their order was better than the Sons of Temperance, because it admitted women on an equal basis. It is now known as the International Order of Good Templars.

The 1st Battalion in Kuldanna, 1904. These men are the hardened drinkers. The three signs at the front of the group, from left to right, read 'Innocents abroad', 'The Kuldanna Arms' and 'The Sun Dodgers, Kuldanna, 1904'. The dog in the centre at the front has a tobacco pipe protruding from its jaws. The regimental magazine later recorded that great steps were taken by the battalion to ensure that the best quality malt liquor was provided (to avoid the men sampling the local liquor) and, although many of the heavy drinkers were beyond the pale, they were encouraged to take their supper in the Royal Army Temperance Association coffee shop in the Murray Hills.

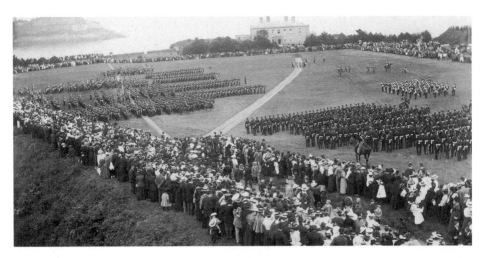

The 2nd Battalion arrived in Guernsey in 1897. The following year they held the Queen's Birthday Parade on 24 May at Belvedere Field. The regimental journal records:

> Long before the appointed time (11.30 a.m.) the spectators began to arrive in their thousands. The proceedings commenced with the usual Royal Salute and *feu-de-joie*, after which our half-battalion trooped the colour, this was the show of the day as far as we were concerned.

Here we see the battalion on that parade together with local militia units.

The band of the 2nd Battalion pictured outside the Royal Engineer's office in Guernsey, *c.*1898. During this posting the band and drums were in great demand. Among their regular concerts was one held at the Town Arsenal on 16 November 1898, stage manager Maj. C.R.M. O'Brien. *The Guernsey Evening Press* reported:

> The fine band of the Wiltshire Regiment, under its efficient bandmaster performed several really good selections... Band Sergeant Smith played a saxaphone solo with his usual ability... Private Quinton gave a piccolo solo in good style. The last piece by the band, a plantation song and chorus, 'Way down dar in Tenessee' was extremely good.

In Guernsey, the 2nd Battalion was stationed in several locations: the Citadel (Fort George), Princes's Lines, Lower Lines, and Fort Jerbourg. The Citadel Barracks contained seven married quarters, accommodation for one company, quartermaster's stores, canteen, grocery bar, tailor's shop, sergeants' mess, billiard room, kitchen and as the regimental magazine recorded, 'we shall all be relieved to hear we have a guardroom and cells'. Alderney, 20 miles away, had accommodation for four companies at Fort Albert. Here we see the company drilling at the Citadel.

A fatigue party from A Company, 2nd Battalion, at the Citadel, Fort George, Guernsey. Fatigues of this type were designed not only to keep the barracks in good order, but also to keep the men occupied. On 20 September 1899 the battalion left Guernsey for Aldershot under the command of Capt. F.S. Picot.

The 1st Battalion, Voluntary Workshops, Quetta, India, 1899. At this time the battalion had to be largely self-sufficient and workshops of this type had multiple benefits. They kept the men occupied, gave them skills that proved useful on demobilisation and the battalion benefited from the tailoring, cobbling, printing and other work. The skills learned in these workshops were particularly useful when the battalion was on the march in India.

B Company 1st Battalion, Quetta, India, 1899 under the command of Capt. G. Rigby (seated centre). This company won the musketry shield for 1898–99. The weather conditions in Quetta varied from extremely hot in the summer to below zero conditions in the winter. The mode of winter dress seen here was introduced to enable these infantry soldiers to operate in adverse conditions and to maintain a presence in the tribal areas.

1st Battalion regimental children's school, Quetta, India, 1899. The schoolmaster was Mr. C. Ross (rear right) and the schoolmistress in charge was Miss A. Barnes (seated right). The schoolmistress was very often married to a non-commissioned officer and travelled with the battalion on its different postings. In addition to schooling the children, assistance was often given to those soldiers who wished to learn to read and write.

The staff of the regimental magazine *The Nines*, Quetta, India, 1899. Edition No.1 appeared in December 1890 under the editorship of Lt Arthur Barnes, who remained its editor and manager for many years. The printing press was purchased from the Leicestershire Regiment in 1889. The magazine was called *The Nines* to reflect the former numerical designation of the 2nd Battalion and was published up to the commencement of the Boer War. Owing to the Boer War, the printing press and accessories were sold and the proceeds used to purchase a cup for cross-country running to be presented to the winning company. This tradition was continued after the regiment's amalgamation with the Royal Berkshires in 1959 to form the Duke of Edinburgh's Royal Regiment, when the Nines Cup was competed for each year.

The winning tent team, India, 1899. Maj. Wyndham later recalled:

> The rank and file were accommodated in tents, sixteen men being allotted to each tent. At each camp, ample supplies of straw had been collected which was used to cover the ground. Each officer was supplied with an 80lb Kabul tent ... usually furnished with a bathroom at the back. All tents had to be aligned properly. The adjutant stood majestically at the top of the broad centre street with his attendant satellites, the sergeant major and orderly bugler, waiting till company orderly sergeants should report all ready. Then came the crucial moment. The sergeant major reports 'all correct'. The adjutant makes a sign to the bugler, and the regimental call, followed by a long 'G' rings out and at the call, the whole mass of big EP tents rise slowly up together, and what was an open plain becomes suddenly a canvas town with streets complete. If any tent is out of line we start again.

The drummers' tent, 1st Battalion, 1901. These soldiers were adept at keeping themselves comfortable in adverse conditions. This team of drummers are the winners of a battalion competition designed to encourage soldiers to keep the tent lines in good order. If the soldiers remained in one location for any length of time, gardens would soon spring up.

Above left: Although not at war, there were nevertheless dangers involved in soldiering on the frontier in India. Here three soldiers of B Company, 1st Battalion, stand at the grave in Jamrud Road Cemetery of a fellow soldier. Pte Patrick James Keohane was shot whilst on sentry duty at Peshawar on 23 February 1901. The grave was erected by his comrades and the inscription reads:

> At his post where the Kyber shadows, pacing to and fro.
> Fearing not the danger, nor the Moslem his hidden foe.
> The gathering dark had deepened, the heart of the night had come
> A flash, a report, then a silence, The ghastly deed was done.
> Stout heart, staunch friend, brave sentinel, borne on our shoulders high.
> Gently to rest we lay thee, but thy mem'ry shall not die.

The dangers continued: the following year on 2 February 1902, a sentry shot and killed a Shinwari rifle thief. Two regimental police were slightly injured during this attack. Most of these attacks came about because local tribesmen needed weapons and the local British garrison was always a good source if the unit had bad discipline. The Wiltshires lost no weapons.

Above right: 1st Battalion, Wiltshire Regiment. A memorial erected by the battalion to commemorate those who died in Quetta between 1895 and 1900. The regimental digest of service recorded that by December 1898 the battalion had lost sixty-seven in that one year alone, with most of the fatalities being caused by enteric fever. At this time, all regiments suffered in the same way and the high death rate did not seem to get more than a passing mention in the regimental records. It is not known if this memorial still exists.

No. 1 Section, D Company, 1st Battalion, India, 1904, the winners of the attack practice. All these soldiers are experienced soldiers with the minimum of six years' service, which is indicated by the inverted chevrons worn on the lower left sleeves. They are all marksmen, which would be reflected by a higher rate of pay. At this time it was said that the Queen's and the Wiltshires were the two best battalions in India. On the first occasion on which the battalion test, drawn up by Lord Kitchener, was introduced, the 1st Battalion obtained the second highest points of any unit in India.

The bayonet fighting team, B Company, 1st Battalion, Rawalpindi, 1904. These soldiers carried out extensive training with the spring-loaded dummy bayonets seen in this photograph. This training clearly paid off when in Karachi they fielded a spring-bayonet fighting team which was victorious against all-comers up to the year 1911. Only the best competitors were selected to represent their company and it was from the winners that battalion teams were formed to take part in army competitions. The 1st Battalion team were Army Winners in India and South Africa for sixteen years in a row. This photograph seems to be unique in depicting the tasselled groin protectors – there are no other images in the regimental collection that shows these items of equipment.

1st Battalion championship runners, India, between 1906-1908. Left to right: Cpl Chandler, Lt & Adj. Guy, Lt-Col. Kirkwood and Pte Pratt. Cpl Chandler was the army champion in India at distances of a mile and over, and Pte Pratt was the army champion runner over a quarter of a mile and the 120-yard sprint. The trophy is the George White Challenge Shield. Lt Guy served in the Boer War and later the First World War when he was awarded a DSO in 1916. Lt-Col. Kirkwood commanded the 2nd Battalion during the Boer War after Col. Carter was wounded.

No. 3 Section B Company, 1st Battalion, with their display of hunting trophies in Dagshai, India, 1906. All ranks were encouraged to shoot. Lt-Col. Wyndham later remembered:

Everyday, as soon as the march was over, all the keen ones went off seeking duck and snipe. One day some of the band, who had gone out with a motley collection of arms, returned in triumph with a fine leopard, which had jumped out of some thick grass. I believe the beast charged them several times, but was met with volleys of all sorts of stuff and was finally slain. As far as I recollect the skin was made into an apron for the Sergeant Drummer.

The opening of the new shooting range for Salisbury and District Rifle Club, by FM Lord Roberts in April 1906. Lord Roberts is in the centre of the photograph at the front of the platform party. The man to the left of him wearing the hat and the spotted tie is Edward Tennant, Liberal MP for Salisbury. The white bearded man on the left of the group on the platform is the Revd Allan Webb, Dean of Salisbury. Lord Radnor Commanding Officer of the 1st Wilts Volunteer Rifle Corps is to the right of Roberts as we look at the photograph. Far right, wearing slouch hats with the Moonrakers badge, are members of a Salisbury contingent of the Wiltshire Volunteer Rifle Corps. The range was in the pleasure gardens, behind what is now Salisbury Library.

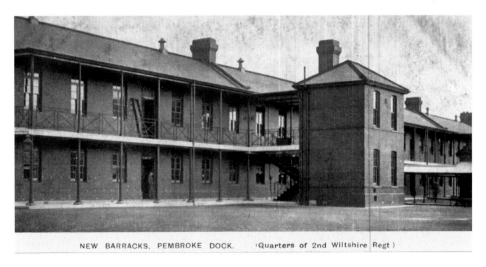

NEW BARRACKS. PEMBROKE DOCK.   ¡Quarters of 2nd Wiltshire Regt)

On 17 October 1905, the 2nd Battalion left Bentley railway station, Hampshire, in two trains and proceeded to Pembroke Dock where it remained for the next three years. Here it received numerous recruits from the Devizes depot, many of whom, after further training, were passed on to the 1st Battalion in India. The barracks at Pembroke Dock were new and considered to be the state of the art. On 7 October 1908, the battalion embarked on SS *Southern* and sailed from Hobbs Point, Pembroke Dock, for Ireland, arriving the same day at Rosslare and left for Dublin, then marched to quarters in Portobello Barracks. Two officers and forty-eight men who had been placed in isolation because of measles were left behind.

Pembroke Dock Barracks, 1906. At this time the soldiers of the 2nd Battalion ate in company locations with the food cooked by battalion cooks who received training at Aldershot. The Army Catering Corps was not formed until 1941. Depending on the type of barracks, meals were usually taken in the same rooms where the soldiers slept.

A fatigue party of the 2nd Battalion in Pembroke Docks. These soldiers are wearing the universally hated and short-lived Broderick caps. Because of the battalion's location at this time the men were often used for coaling ships. This photograph is believed to have been taken just before one of these coaling exercises.

The warrant officers and sergeants of the 2nd Battalion at Pembroke Dock, between 1905–08. Sgt-Maj. Sydney Grant, DCM (sitting fifth from right) was a Boer War veteran who had won his Distinguished Conduct Medal in that conflict. He was later commissioned and after retirement became a leading figure in the Regimental Association.

The officers' mess staff, 2nd Battalion, Pembroke Dock, between 1905–08. The officers' mess was run along country house lines and the officers' mess servants, all serving soldiers, normally doubled up as officers' batmen [servants]. Here we see the table made up with much of the regimental silver for a function. Although not visible in this photograph, the battalion's Colours were kept in the officers' mess.

The Wiltshire Regiment Volunteers pictured at Devizes after returning from Bisley where they won the All England Championships in 1896. Standing, left to right: Cpl Hedley, a nurseryman from Devizes, Pte Fred Springford, who owned a cycle shop, Pte King from Bromham and Lt E.L. Anstie, chairman of Wiltshire Education Committee and of E. & W. Anstie Ltd the tobacco manufacturers. Seated, centre: Pte King and his brother Pte King and Sgt F.G. Billingham, Devizes Borough Surveyor. Front row: L/Cpl John Harding, who worked on the Roundway Estate, Lt Albert Randle, a Devizes architect (he became the regimental depot adjutant during the Boer War) and L/Cpl Gilbert from Wilcot, who was one of the best shots in the country.

The official opening of the Wiltshire Regiment cottages, 24 November 1904. They are located just opposite Le Marchant Barracks, Devizes. The ceremony was performed by the Countess of Pembroke. These cottages were for the benefit of retired, and in many cases war injured, old soldiers of the regiment. The Welfare State was yet to come into being and the regiment had to look after its own, albeit in a restricted way.

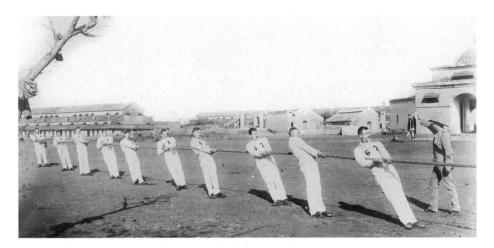

The 1st Battalion tug-of-war team taking the strain. After the Crimean War, the value of exercise and competition became recognised for the first time in the army and both Wiltshire battalions made a name for themselves towards the end of the nineteenth century, maintaining this reputation into the twentieth. The 1st Battalion in India fielded tug-of-war teams of some excellence, winning everything in sight from 1901 through to 1911. When the battalion went to South Africa they continued to win trophies.

The 1st Battalion heavyweight tug-of-war team, Amballa, Punjab, India, 1907. They were the winners of the Calcutta Shield open to all India for the years 1905, 1906 and 1907, also outright winners of Lady Minto's cup, again open to all India in 1907. In addition they were winners at Peshawar 1901–02 and Rawalpindi 1904–05. Standing, left to right: Bdsm Spackman, Pte Gardner, Sgt Palmer (trainer), L/Cpl Dove and Pte Oram. Sitting: Pte Trimnell, Sgt Carter, Lt C. Carter, Lt-Col. Kirkwood, DSO, Lt & Adj. Guy, Ptes Stagg and Carter.

The 1st Battalion motor pool, Dublin, 1908–10. The use of this transport was very much restricted to the senior officers of the battalion on official business. For the rest of the battalion it was business as usual with route marches being taken each week. It was here in 1909 at the sergeants' annual dinner that Sgt-Maj. Wickens, QM Sgt Bance and Col-Sgt Hewitt proposed that a Wiltshire Regiment Old Comrades Association be formed. The idea was developed over the next year and the Association was officially formed in 1910.

The 3rd Militia Battalion on parade in Le Marchant Barracks on the presentation of Colours in 1913. The 3rd Militia Battalion originally had its headquarters in Bath Road, Devizes; these were handed over to the County Constabulary in 1880 when the militia moved to the new barracks. Both the militia and regular recruits lived together in the same barrack rooms, and were treated alike except for the amount of drill instruction. One year after this parade, the First World War started and the barracks put into practice a well-rehearsed mobilisation plan with the dress uniforms worn in this photograph being returned to the stores.

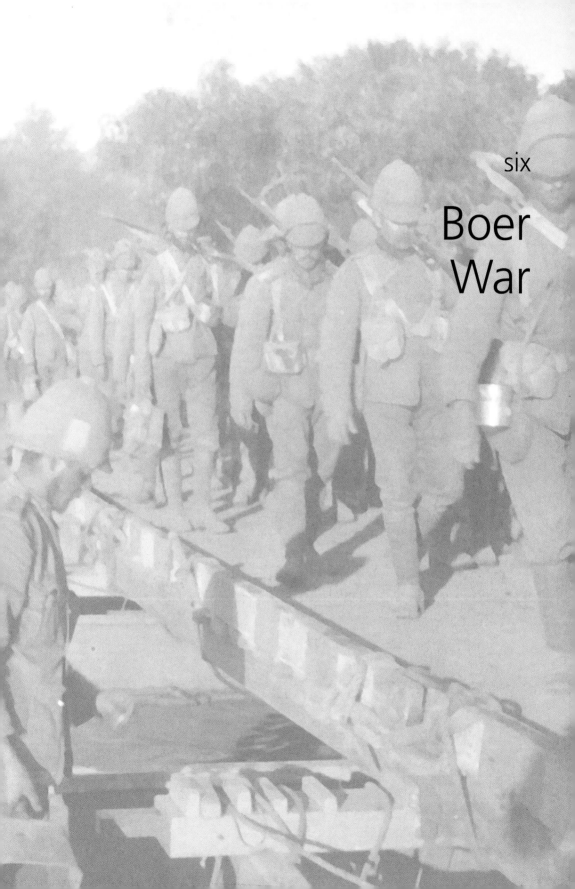

six

Boer
War

The mounted infantry section, 2nd Battalion, pictured here shortly before embarkation on 22 October 1899. They sailed from Southampton on the SS *Orient* ahead of the rest of the battalion, who followed on 16 December the same year. These soldiers are still wearing the scarlet jackets with white facings, which were replaced by khaki uniforms on embarkation. The officer seated in the centre is Lt A.H. Hutton-Wilson, who remained with the section for the Boer War. During the First World War he served on the staff, being awarded the DSO. He retired in 1928 and died in 1955.

Officers, 2nd Battalion, before their departure for South Africa to take part in the Boer War. Rear row, standing left to right: QM A. Yardley, Capt. E. Vincent, Lt H. Rogers (died), Capt. L. Holmes-a-Court, Lts C. Thornton (wounded at Rensburg), Tacky and M. Richards, Capt. W. Matcham and Maj. F. Picot. Second row, sitting: Lt E. Henslow, Majs Macmullen (died of wounds) and Beatson (wounded), Lt-Col. H. Carter (wounded), Lt & Adj. E. Evans (wounded) and Maj. Stock (prisoner of war). Front row, sitting: Lt Mellish (died), Capt. W. Bolton (wounded), Lts R. Gillson and Winstanley.

The 2nd Battalion embarked for South Africa at Southampton on 16 December 1899 on the hired transport *Gascon*. The battalion, under the command of Lt-Col. Carter, was 817 strong, four of whom died en route. Several days later another 262 men followed on the ship *America* with both units meeting up at Naaupoort Camp. Sgt Blencowe later recalled:

The other unit on the *Gascon* was the Royal Irish Regiment who were not well stocked… so the Wilts shared their fare with the destitute Irishmen. This was repaid some time later at Stormberg when the Royal Irish received thirty-six Barrels of Guinness as a present; they sent eighteen barrels over to the Wilts.

Maj. H. Stock, 2nd Battalion on-board *Gascon* en route to South Africa. He was in command of D Company. In February 1900 the 2nd Battalion joined the 12th Brigade and were engaged in holding the left wing of the Colesburg position with 1,700 men against some 6,000 Boers. On the withdrawal of the brigade, two companies of the Wiltshires were cut off and surrounded. After a fighting withdrawal the companies had fifty-seven men killed or wounded and ninety-one captured, with only three escaping. Maj. Stock was the senior surviving officer who was captured. He was later subjected to an enquiry at which he stated that Maj. Macmullen had received an order to bring his men to a position indicated, and that the start would take place at 5 a.m. on the following morning. At 3.34 a.m. a patrol was sent out to communicate with the main outpost line, but it returned and reported that no one was to be seen. The companies were then formed up and marched to the base camp, and on finding it deserted, started at once for Arundel in extended formation. Almost immediately, they were attacked from the left rear by a body of about 350 Boers. In the open plain there was absolutely no cover. They were then outflanked by a further force of 600 Boers and forty mounted men. The enquiry completely exonerated him. He retired after the war.

Officers, 2nd Battalion, Bloemfontein, South Africa, in March 1900. Rear row, left to right: ADC to Gen. Clements, Lts Folkestone, Matcham, Wimberley and Rogers, Capts L. Holmes-a-Court, Bolton, Evans (wounded) and Woodbourne, -?- and Capt. Luce. Middle row: Capts Brown and Oxley, Maj. Kirkwood, Gen. Clements, Lt-Col. Carter, Maj. Beatson, Capts Moody and Broadbridge. Sitting: Lts Barker, Fisher, Nicholson, Gillson and Yardley and Volunteer Officer -?-.

A Mr Pepper from Salisbury of the National Scottish Red Cross stationed at Kroonstead regularly wrote articles for the Wiltshire papers and he was constantly on the lookout for 'The Wilts Boys', as he described them. One day he sighted them and recorded it in the following terms:

> This morning at breakfast we noticed large body of men, horses and wagons were coming over the hills towards us. Then opened up to our view was the engrossing sight of the Wiltshires advancing in full battle array, with skirmishers thrown out some distance across the veldt, then came then came the main body. Not the well-fed, spick and span troops we may have seen passing through Salisbury to some review but thin, gaunt, bearded men in ragged, dirty, soiled khaki – thin from living on biscuits for eighty-two days, but, nevertheless, wiry-looking, and hard as nails. They were tanned as brown as leather by a tropical sun.

This is one of many photographs of the 2nd Battalion taken on the march by Lt Mellish.

Another photograph of the 2nd Battalion marching across the apparently never ending South African veldt. Marching and manning outposts took up most of the time. Sgt Blencowe later recalled:

> The following day the regiment were detailed to prolong the line to the left, and we had to march about ten miles to a place called Madder's Farm, and it being a very hot day, and our first march in the country since coming off the ship, it went very stiff, and at that time we were carrying our greatcoats, which made things worse. Rejoining my section I found them venting their opinion of marching in the heat of the day, in no very uncertain terms.

Here we see soldiers of the 2nd Battalion marching across a pontoon, again photographed by Lt Mellish. Lt-Col. Carter later recounted:

> We spanned the Orange River by pontoon bridge at Steekenstroom's Drift and crossed unopposed on 17th March. The Regiment dug all the screened approaches to the river for the pontoons, and also a road for, and dragged six guns up a hill (Devizes Hill) 400ft high, to cover the crossing, working all night at this task.

2nd Battalion officers' cart, normally driven by locally recruited drivers, following up the marching troops. This photograph is very unusual as it shows one soldier with a pushbike. Lt-Col. Carter later wrote, 'We marched to Smaldell through Winburg, some sixty miles. There were no mounted men with Gen. Rundle's force, so the Wiltshire cyclists, twenty-five in number, did all the scouting to the front, taking some prisoners.' As a result of the lack of mounted troops Capt. Matcham, assisted by Sgt Hart, organised a few scouts and mounted them on captured Boer ponies. These became known as Matcham's Horse.

Officers' mess batmen of the 2nd Battalion prepare their officers' meals at the end of a day's march. An examination of the diaries that have survived show that many soldiers were quite happy to take on this task because of the perks, in this case extra food. All this equipment was carried in the cart shown above. The uniforms worn during this campaign quickly deteriorated as Sgt Blencowe remembered:

> A pretty disreputable looking lot of soldiers we were too, personally I was pretty well off, only showing my knees and socks, John had sewn a big piece of sugar sack across his backside, which was all the more interesting as it had 'sugar' in big letters across it and underneath 8olbs, honourable clothes indeed.

Lt Lawrence Oliver Falaise Mellish, 2nd Battalion, who photographed the battalion, was born in January 1876 and educated at St Paul's School. A good cricketer and an all-round athlete, he joined the Wiltshire Regiment in May 1897 and attended a signalling course at Aldershot in 1898. Prior to the battalion embarking for South Africa he had the honour, together with Lt Gillson, of marching the battalion's Colours to the Devizes Barracks for safe keeping. In December 1899 he went with the battalion to South Africa and served in the Colesburg operations and the subsequent advance from the north of Cape Colony. He died of enteric fever at Bloemfontein on 2 June 1900. The battalion lost ninety-two soldiers to disease during the Boer War.

A Maxim gun team of the 2nd Battalion in action near Norvals Pont during the Boer War. The battalion was based at this location several times during the war and was always on the alert for attacks by Boer commandos. Norvals Pont also consisted of a concentration area for Boer prisoners and their families, and was a main part of the railway system. The substantial bridge there was blown up by the Boers on 6 March 1900.

The Volunteer Service Company formed up on the square at Le Marchant Barracks, Devizes, *c.*1900. Pte Rodda, 2nd Volunteer Battalion, later recorded:

On the 13 January the New Swindon contingent were formally inspected for fitness by Surgeon-Capt. Swinhoe and were attested by J. Brown Magistrate assisted by Col-Sgt Osbourne. Most of this unit were members of the Great Western Railway. We went to Devizes Barracks and measured up for uniform. Had drill and rifle practice and were lectured by Maj. Picot on scouting and outpost duties. We were photographed on the 13 February after being inspected by the Duke of Somerset and then went to Southampton on 16 February. We were provided with refreshment from the 'Absent minded beggars fund'. [Financed by public contributions this provided comforts for the troops.]

The Salisbury contingent of the Wiltshire Volunteer Service Company pose for a photograph prior to making their way to Devizes to join their comrades from other parts of Wiltshire. Some of these men would have had military experience in regular units, but in the main, these were volunteers who gave up their weekends to train. On arrival in South Africa the volunteer company became J Company of the 2nd Battalion. They removed the 'V' (signifying them as volunteers) from helmets and shoulder straps.

The Wiltshire Volunteer Service officers, senior warrant officers and sergeants on-board ship en route to South Africa to join the 2nd Battalion. Standing, left to right: Sgt Thomas, Col-Sgt Yardley, Lt Luce (died of disease), Maj. Folkestone, Sgt Harding (died of enteric fever 13 May 1900), Lt Kendle and Sgt Booker. Sitting: Sgts Gough and Elwood (slightly wounded at Slapkrantz, July 1900).

Lt Luce is remembered on the Malmesbury Memorial which reads: 'To the glory of God and in memory of Walter Cecil Luce, Lieutenant of the Volunteer Service Company of the Wiltshire Regiment. Born 27 November 1873. Died at Springfontein South Africa, 11 February 1901'.

No.1 Section, Volunteer Company, 2nd Battalion Wiltshire Regiment. Back row, left to right: Ptes Cornish, Humphries, Silcox and Sturgess, Cpl Hart, Ptes Stokes and Ferris. Second row: Sgt Thorne, Ptes Smith, Green and Brown, Lt Kendle, Randell, Cornish, Randell and Sgt Dawes. Front row: –?–, Cpl Davis, –?–, Randell, Smith, Smith and Rawlings. Sgt Dawes was later commissioned into the Wiltshire Regiment. He went to France on the outbreak of the First World War and was the first officer of the 1st Battalion to be killed in action.

THE WILTSHIRE REGIMENT.
3RD BATTN

KILWORTH CAMP.
GALE & POLDEN L.TD REG.D DESIGN.

In 1900 the Wiltshire 3rd (Militia) Battalion were embodied for the South African War. They were chosen for this role as at that time they were only four men under strength. They initially went to Ireland, then to St Helena in the South Atlantic to guard Boer prisoners of war. A number of underage or medically downgraded regular soldiers were also attached to the militia battalion. Here we see a postcard sent from the 3rd (Militia) Battalion in Ireland 1900.

A postcard showing the arrival of the Wiltshire 3rd (Militia) Battalion on St Helena making their way to Deadwood Camp. They arrived on 6 July 1901 relieving the soldiers of the 3rd and 4th Gloucestershire Militia Battalions who embarked on the troopship *Mohawk* for home.

Soldiers of the 3rd Battalion march a working party of Boer prisoners from Deadwood Camp. The Boer farmers were proud men whose relationship with the British guards was very good. One of Gen. Cronje's bodyguards, Job Cordier, later recalled, 'Man, they can say what they like, but the English were damn good to us'. The chance of escape was very remote, but nevertheless the guards had to adopt a high profile, with the main danger to both the prisoners and guards coming from disease. Between 1900 and 1902 a total of 6,000 prisoners were sent to St Helena with a death rate of only 3 per cent. In all 175 Boers are buried on the island.

When not guarding prisoners the soldiers of the 3rd Battalion were employed on all manner of fatigues. This was necessary to maintain a decent standard of living and at the same time ensured idle hands were kept busy. Here we see a group of soldiers moving house in the Deadwood Camp area. They remained on the island for a year and after their return to Wiltshire the battalion was awarded the honour St Helena to be carried on their Colours, as well as being inscribed on the cross of their badge.

Above left: Capt. William Atkins, 2nd Battalion, was born in June 1861 and after service of six years in the ranks was appointed second lieutenant in the Royal Irish Rifles in July 1888. He was later promoted into the Wiltshire Regiment as a captain in July 1896 and commanded G Company in Guernsey and Alderney in 1897. He did not go to South Africa with the main body of the battalion but followed later, joining the mounted infantry, with which he saw much service, eventually commanding it. He was present at Rensburg, the relief of Kimberley, the pursuit and capture of Cronje (a Boer general) and in every action up to the taking of Pretoria, including battles at Jacobsdal, Diamond Hill and Sannas Post. Whilst serving in the 2nd Mounted Infantry he was killed in action at Nooitgedact on 13 December 1900.

This photograph gives a clear picture of the equipment worn by officers at this time. He is almost modelling the equipment for the Army order No. 151 of November 1898 which authorised the wearing of the universal pattern Sam Brown belt. The 2nd Battalion digest of service described it as follows:

> The belt is of brown leather 2½ins wide, fastened round the waist in front by a brass buckle. The sword which has a brown leather scabbard with a steel shoe is carried in a frog on the left side. Two braces are provided which cross behind and eventually support the weight of articles carried on the belt, revolver, holster, ammunition pouch and galloping strap completing the equipment.

Above right: Maj. Francis Richard Macmullen, 2nd Battalion, was born May 1855 and entered the 62nd Foot from the West Essex Militia in August 1877. He served in the Egyptian War during 1882 and took part in the action at Kassasin, and the Battle of Tel-el-Kebir. Later employed in the Army Pay Department he subsequently became the adjutant of the 2nd Volunteer Battalion East Yorkshire Regiment. He rejoined the 2nd Battalion in 1899 and proceeded with it to South Africa, taking over command of G Company from Capt. Atkins.

He commanded his company at Rensburg on 15 February 1900, when they were cut off during a major Boer attack. The digest of service reads, 'They eventually took up a position on some low kopjes twenty miles east of the railway and there held out gallantly until they lost a third of their number in killed and wounded including Major Macmullen.' The two Wiltshire companies held their ground against 1,500 Boers which included the crack shots of the Zuid Afrikaanse Republiek Polisie (ZARP). From the reports of the Boers themselves Maj. Macmullen conducted the fight with consummate skill and coolness. Had he not died of his wounds, the result might possibly have been different. The soldiers who were killed in this action were buried where they fell.

Maj. Herbert Thomas de Carteret Hobbs joined the 62nd Foot in 1875. He spent most of his service in the 1st Battalion, becoming the Inspector of Musketry for the battalion. He commanded the 2nd Battalion Wiltshire Volunteers in the years leading up to the Boer War. Based in Chippenham, he brought the battalion up to a high degree of efficiency. On the outbreak of the Boer War there were no vacancies in his regiment for officers so he gained a position in the 1st Battalion West Yorkshire Regiment, going to South Africa with them. He was quickly engaged against the Boers and was captured at the Battle of Beacon Hill whilst trying to save a wounded soldier. During his captivity he came into contact with many of his old Wiltshire Regiment comrades, most of whom had been captured at Rensburg, including Maj. Stock. When they were released they were formed into an ad-hoc battalion under Col. Bullock of the Devons. Maj. Hobbs became the second in command.

The composite battalion of released prisoners of war were en route in an armoured train to Honing Spruit to take up outpost duties when the railway track was blown up and the train ambushed on 22 June 1900. The Boers called on them to surrender but these men had no intention of returning to Boer captivity. They were armed with old Boer rifles and put up a spirited defence until relieved. Maj. Hobbs was hit in the chest and is shown in the centre of this contemporary illustration slumped over a rock after being shot. He was later buried at Kroonstad. In July a memorial service was held at Chippenham in Wiltshire, arranged by the 2nd Volunteer Battalion. It was said that had the government asked for the 2nd Battalion Volunteers to mobilise for the Boer War under Maj. Hobbs every man would have followed him.

Wiltshire Regiment builders of the White Horse, Naval Hill, Bloemfontein, South Africa. A number of people and units have laid claim to the construction of the horse located on the hill behind this group, but research identifies these men as responsible, between the 4 April 1900 and 14 May 1900 when the battalion were based here on outpost duty. The battalion was joined here by Lord Folkestone and the volunteer company who contributed manpower for the task. This area was also a large remount camp and the White Horse was used as a direction finder for troops coming in from the veldt.

Three soldiers of the 2nd Battalion, during the Boer War. In the centre is Pte George Henry Greenman of D Company, who came from Box, near Chippenham, Wiltshire. He joined the regiment in 1892, serving in England and India. Discharged on 14 November 1896 he re-enlisted two weeks later, joining the 2nd Battalion in South Africa. On 20 August 1900 at Waterval, near Hamman's Kraul, the battalion advanced to an attack and had to move through some very thick bush. At the end of the engagement the battalion had suffered one killed and five wounded, one of whom was Pte Greenman. Injured when a bullet passed through his left ear and down to his shoulder, he was saved from a more serious wound by the brass rivets on his shoulder strap deflecting the bullet which went into his haversack and exploded, nearly blowing it to pieces. After his wound was dressed by a comrade he was taken to the nearby Hamman's Kraul Hotel. He was discharged in 1901 and died in 1941, aged seventy-four, a retired stone quarrier. Pte Greenman had two brothers, one of whom served in the 2nd Battalion Royal Berkshire Regiment.

A section of the 2nd Battalion in their blockhouse near Pietermaritzburg, a system devised by Kitchener. By May 1902 there were over 8,000 blockhouses covering 3,700 miles, gradually trapping the Boer guerrillas. These were manned by 50,000 white troops and 16,000 African scouts. The Boer leader, De Wet, claimed the system did not worry him. He called it the 'blockhead' system, and reckoned it extended the war by three months. Sgt Blencowe remembered:

> The duty in these miniature forts was, after our trekking, comparatively easy. We had eight men not including myself and besides finding a sentry continually, and keeping the place clean we had nothing to do, my duty simply consisted in being with the sentry on his post from 3 o'clock in the morning until daybreak.

Sgt Blencowe survived the war with his only injury being a snake bite inflicted whilst on an outpost duty.

Capt. Henry Paton Rogers joined the 1st Battalion from Sandhurst in 1894, later exchanging to the 2nd Battalion in 1895. En route to South Africa and after arrival he was a regular contributor to Wiltshire newspapers, using the name 'Moonraker'. His articles kept local people (many of whom had relations in the battalion) up to date with his unit's activities. In his last letter, printed in August 1900, he wrote:

> It is with great regret that I have to say that we have lost a lot of men from enteric fever. The water is very bad, owing to the Boers having cut our supply at the waterworks. We have lost up to the time of writing about twelve NCOs and men, including orderly room Sgt Pinnock and Sgt Burchell. We have about 150 sick in hospital, mainly enteric fever.

By the time the article appeared in the newspaper Capt. Rogers himself had succumbed to enteric fever, dying on 13 May 1900. He was buried at Bloemfontein.

Maj. Wilfred Nash Bolton joined the Regiment in 1883. He was an instructor in fortifications and gymnastics at the Royal Military College, Sandhurst from 1892 until 1899. He was an international rugby player being capped for Scotland eleven times. An article in the magazine *Field* entitled 'Giants of Rugby of the Past' referred to him as 'one of the strongest men I have ever known. In a match against Scotland Bolton picked up his opponent (Reid) and threw him over the ropes, with the result that he (Reid) never played again'. He was a good hurdler, sprinter and a fine gymnast. He went to South Africa in command of F Company, and at Slabbert's Nek on 12 July 1900 he led the battalion along a goat track on the side of a precipice in fog and went round the enemy left flank, coming in behind the Boers who departed in a hurry. One month later he was wounded at Hamman's Kraul. He appears to have had some legal training as he acted as the prosecutor in the trial of Lt 'Breaker' Morant of the Bushveldt Carabineers for killing Boer prisoners of war. Lt Morant was found guilty and later executed. After the war, Maj. Bolton was appointed as the resident magistrate in Cyprus. He retired in 1905.

Naauwpoort was garrisoned by the 2nd Battalion on a number of occasions during the Boer War. It was described as a small insignificant little place as regards its size and appearance, the buildings all being made of galvanized iron. At that time it was of strategic importance, being one of the supply bases and also the junction with De Aar which connects the Pretoria line with Cape Town and Port Elizabeth. Lt-Col. Carter recorded that the battalion furnished companies from Naauwpoort for various duties wherever assistance might be required against roving bands of the enemy, which constantly threatened the railway and our detached posts. This photograph shows the battalion's tent lines with an ornate regimental badge laid out in whitewashed stones. The battalion still referred to themselves as The Nines, the pre-1881 designation.

seven

March to War

The 1st Battalion during autumn manoeuvres, 30 August 1893, seen here on Crookham Common, Berkshire, at the start of a twenty-mile route march. *The Nines* recorded:

> Reveille sounded at 3.30 a.m., the camp was pretty well astir before that, as all cooks and pioneers left at 4 a.m. The morning broke cloudy and very like rain, the wise ones said it was bound to pelt with rain, as they heard the peacocks in the early morn.

Headed by the band, the 1st Battalion commence the route march. The battalion consisted of five companies and marched and countermarched over what is now West Berkshire. At one point they went into Wiltshire where the sergeants were entertained by the sergeants of the Volunteer Battalion. The routine was fifty minutes of marching followed by ten minutes of rest.

A foot inspection of the 1st Battalion during the autumn manoeuvres of 1893. On average this battalion marched twenty miles per day and a foot inspection at the end of each day ensured blister problems were addressed early. As a consequence the fall out rate remained very low.

Led by the CO, the battalion makes its way along a country road near the Uffington White Horse five miles from Farringdon, Berkshire. Whilst on these manoeuvres the battalion camped at Uffington and Liddington, returning to Aldershot on 19 September 1893. Two years later the battalion sailed for India.

The 1st Battalion rest on the march in India in the 1890s. Lt-Col. Wyndham later remembered:

> We used to march at 5 a.m., and the chief thing which remains fixed in my memory was an eclipse of the moon which was going on one morning, and which caused much discussion in the ranks as to what the ------ had become of the ---- moon? I was carrying the Regimental Colour in the centre of the column which was no joke in those days; the Colour itself of course, was no light burden on a fifteen mile march. In addition, one had to march strictly to attention the whole way, the escort with fixed bayonets.

A posed photograph showing piquets of the 1st Battalion in India, 1897. Whilst on the march into hostile territory it was the tactic of the day to dominate the high ground to ensure the main body were not ambushed. It was called Khud climbing and involved a high degree of fitness. This photograph gives a clear impression of the numbers involved and the type of terrain to be traversed. In a real situation, the soldiers who were sky lined would soon pay the price against the local tribesmen who were skilled at using the ground and were outstanding shots.

The 1st Battalion pause for a group photograph whilst on a route march on the North West Frontier, November 1898. When on the march, infantry battalions in effect became small mobile towns. Unlike England, where public houses sometimes provided ale, in this environment the threat of disease due to drinking bad water was very real as the casualty returns all too often showed.

The 1st Battalion on manoeuvres in India, 1899. Here they have formed a square behind an earth emplacement. Although the British Army, including the 2nd Battalion, were being taught lessons in open warfare by the sharpshooting Boer commandos in South Africa, the troops in the rest of the British Empire were still very much operating to the traditional square. Against lightly armed tribesmen the amount of fire-power coming from such a formation was extremely deadly. Some of these soldiers are wearing the cold weather caps.

The 1st Battalion on the march during the Quetta Manoeuvres in 1899, headed by Gen. Hart, VC. Lady Hart is also in the party. The conditions for the footsore Wiltshire infantrymen behind had not changed for a century, which Rudyard Kipling summed up as follows:

> So 'ark an' 'eed you rookies, which is always grumblin' sore'
> There's worser things than marchin' from Umballa to Cawnpore;
> An' if your 'eels are blistered an' they feels to 'urt like 'ell,
> You drop some tallow in your socks an' that will make 'em well.

The 1st Battalion rest during the 1899 Quetta Manoeuvres. These soldiers were well used to the steady and relentless marching pace with a ten-minute rest every hour. The band and drums still carried and played their instruments on these marches. Note the drummer boy at the front.

The Maxim gun section of the 1st Battalion, Dagshai, India, 1907. At this time each infantry battalion had two machine-guns. Training was very important as a journal recorded in the 1890s that the guns 'jammed at Ulundi, jammed at Dogali, they jammed at Abu Klea and Tofrek, and in some cases with unfortunate results'. The Maxim machine-gun was adopted by the British Army in 1889. The gun was first used by Britain's colonial forces in the Matabele War in 1893–94. In one engagement, fifty soldiers fought off 5,000 Matabele warriors with just four Maxim guns.

The 1st Battalion changed over to the 1908 equipment whilst in India, taking this photograph to record the event. The soldiers on the right show the new equipment. In spite of the introduction of a new style in 1903, the Slade Wallace equipment that was heavily criticised during the Boer War, because of the loss of ammunition from the inadequate pouches, continued in service until replaced in 1908.

In 1909 the battalion left India for South Africa. One of the lessons from the Boer War was to have the ability to dig fast and deep. Here soldiers of the 1st Battalion rest during a trench-digging exercise in 1910. They had yet to learn the art of constructing a trench system in such a way that one shell landing in the trench would not inflict blast damage in a straight line. Four years later these soldiers would be digging in on the Western Front.

The 1st Battalion crossing the the Umsindusi River during one of the many exercises whilst stationed in South Africa. The battalion arrived in Pietermaritzburg in 1909, remaining until 1913 when it returned to England. This was very much a garrison posting with great emphasis placed on sport and fitness. The battalion continued to excel at tug-of-war and bayonet fighting. Great pride was taken in its marching ability, which was practised frequently.

Another view of the same river which in good weather was fordable but in adverse weather conditions could prove fatal, as was shown in 1910. The Commander-in-Chief Gen. Lord Methuen supervised a major exercise where the 1st Battalion were to carry out an attack on a militia camp. As the battalion secretly advanced a storm blew up, leaving the men, who were only in light marching order, wet to the skin. As a result Lord Methuen decided to abandon the exercise and return the troops to barracks. But by the time this order was received the Umsindusi River and tributaries were raging torrents. The local paper reported:

> Just after the head of the column had crossed the first drift, the Spruit came down in a huge wave. One man [Pte Drew] was immediately swept away before the eyes of his comrades who were quite powerless to help him, and two others were subsequently found missing. One hundred men were trapped and many acts of gallantry were performed, avoiding further fatalities.

Fort Napier, a memorial erected over the graves of Pte Newport, Pte Drew (right) and Pte Clay who were drowned on the exercise. L/Cpl A. Hindn who had carved the regiment's badge into the rock at Cherat in 1902 assisted in constructing the monument.

A section of the 1st Battalion form up to take part in an attack during exercises in South Africa, *c.*1910. Although bunched up in this photograph, the lessons of the Boer War were practised, in particular keeping plenty of space between soldiers when advancing to the attack. Four years later many of these men would be in action for real against the German Army, where they inflicted great damage with their Lee Enfield rifles as seen in this photograph. These men shot for their pay and the expectation was fifteen well aimed shots a minute.

The band of the 1st Wiltshire Volunteer Rifle Corps march into Lulworth Camp on 3 August 1907, led by the bandmaster, F.W. Carter. He was born in Salisbury in 1860, joining the volunteers at the age of fourteen. He was later promoted to band sergeant, followed by a further promotion to bandmaster. On the outbreak of the First World War he formed the band of the 2nd/4th Battalion, going with that battalion to India, where he served throughout the war. After the war he was responsible for re-forming the 4th Battalion band, remaining until 1934 when he retired after sixty years' service.

The 4th Battalion march off after de-training at Ludgershall in 1909. This was on the occasion of their first annual camp as the 4th Battalion, having been merged from the two Volunteer Battalions under the Haldane reforms of the army in 1908. After the amalgamation the company locations were reduced to Malmesbury, Devizes, Swindon, Salisbury, Trowbridge, Bradford-on-Avon, Warminster and Wilton. Note the slouch hats, the wearing of which was discontinued shortly afterwards.

The 2nd Battalion marching through Wilton, near Salisbury, September 1899, during the field state manoeuvres which were commanded by Gen. Sir Redvers Buller, VC. The battalion, under the command of Lt-Col. Harford, was in the 8th Brigade of the 4th Division. This exercise consisted of 24,729 men, 4,653 horses and 725 wagons and carts. Afterwards the battalion left from Salisbury railway station to make its way back to Guernsey.

The 2nd Battalion march past the King of Spain in review order on 8 June 1905, at Bordon, Hampshire. The battalion was stationed at Longmore Camp and reviews of this type were common during this period. The year before, on 10 June, the battalion had marched in review past His Imperial Highness the Archduke Frederick of Austria. On 11 January 1905 an army order, dated 21 December 1904, authorised the Duke of Edinburgh's (Wiltshire Regiment) to display the honour South Africa 1899–1902 on Colours and Appointments.

On 7 October 1908, the 2nd Battalion embarked on the SS *Southern* and sailed from Hobbs Point, Pembroke Dock, for Ireland. They arrived the same day at Rosslare, travelled by train to Dublin, then marched to quarters in Portobello Barracks. Shown here are the Corps of Drums of the 2nd Battalion in Ireland around 1910, leading the battalion back to Portobello Barracks after a church parade.

The band, drums and Colours of the 2nd Battalion on parade in Dublin, Ireland, on St Patrick's Day, 17 March 1911. The battalion arrived here in 1908, remaining until 1910. Most of the time was taken up with musketry, route marching and sport, although high-profile parades such as the one seen here required a lot of preparation. The days of wearing full dress uniforms as shown in this photograph were numbered as the First World War approached

The Officers of the 2nd Battalion, Gosport, 6 January 1913, prior to embarkation for Gibraltar. Rear row, left to right: Lts Burroughs, Beaver (commanded 2nd Battalion 1933), Hill (killed in action, 8 July 1916) and Wallis, Capt. Moore, 2nd-Lts Shelford (wounded) and Macnamara, Lt Smith and QM Lt Martin. Centre row: Lt Herry, Majs Wyndham (prisoner of war and commanded 2nd Battalion 1919) and Forbes (prisoner of war), Lt-Col. Jeffries (commanded 6th Battalion 1915), Capt. & Adj. Culver, Capts Stoddart (killed in action 27 October 1914) and Coddington. Front row: Lt Martyn (missing in action 21 March 1918), 2nd-Lts Grimston (killed in action 21 October 1914) and Down.

The two regular battalions rarely met. They did meet in February 1913 when the 1st Battalion called at Gibraltar on their way home from South Africa. Here 300 officers and men transferred to the 2nd Battalion, who at that time were garrisoning the Rock. Here we see nine of those men, referred to as The Turnovers, at Catalin Bay, Gibraltar. Many friendships were rekindled and much beer drunk. The regimental history records, 'Capt. Rowan, the 62nd's Adjutant, paraded the drums, which played the 1st Battalion's Regimental March to extricate the laggards and lead them back to the ship'.

The officers of the 1st Battalion, Jellalabad Barracks, Tidworth, 1913. Back row, left to right: Lts D.H. Goodhart and W.C. Loder-Symonds (wounded and captured, escaped and later killed in action with Royal Flying Corps), 2nd-Lt L.J. Fairchild (Adjutant 7th Battalion 1915), Lt K.J.P. Oliphant (prisoner of war), Capt. W.I. Cordon, 2nd-Lt C.C. Morse, Lts J.H.M. Mee (commanded 1st Battalion 1932), G.S. Browne (wounded), R.H. Broome and L.B. Green (Adjutant 6th Battalion 1915). Sitting: Capts H.B. Fisher, F.W. Stoddart (killed in action 27 October 1914) and M.C. Richards, Maj. T. Roche (killed in action 17 November 1914), Lt-Col. A.W Hasted (wounded), Capts P.S. Rowen (wounded), M.L. Formby, W.A. Blake (awarded DSO 1915) and W. Dawes (killed in action 23 August 1914).

Soldiers of the 1st Battalion present arms at the civic reception at Devizes on 3 March 1913, having arrived home from South Africa with Maj. Hasted in command. The battalion had been on foreign service for seventeen and a half years. It was recorded at the time that the battalion returned with nineteen men who had served abroad with the battalion for the whole of that period; in addition six of these soldiers were already in India serving in the 2nd battalion in 1894 and stayed with the 1st for the remainder of the tour.

The reception was held at the Corn Exchange. Decorations were by Messrs C.E. Neate & Sons and the gallery was handsomely draped in scarlet and buff. The ladies had decorated the tables tastefully with spring flowers and the first course was already laid out for the men, who were quite ready to begin. The band of the 3rd Battalion played throughout and it was recorded that this was the largest sit-down dinner ever taken at Devizes. After long speeches the buglers sounded fall in, and the regiment marched back to the railway station en route for Tidworth.

In June 1913 the 1st Battalion, stationed at Tidworth, took part in a march throughout the county. They visited Devizes, Swindon, Chippenham, Melksham, Trowbridge, Warminster and finally Salisbury, receiving a civic reception at each town. As the battalion entered Salisbury a change of arrangements meant that the Wiltshires arrived at the junction of the Wilton and Devizes Roads before the schoolchildren had assembled. But as the *Salisbury Journal* reported, 'The Colonel kindly called a halt while the scholars were informed of the invasion and the children tumbled out with their teachers.' Here we see the Wiltshires, led by the band of the 4th Battalion under Sgt Dmr Neville, marching through the city centre.

The battalion passes the Market House (now the library), Salisbury, and turns into Castle Street, en route to Victoria Park, where it was to camp for the night. It then returned to the Market House for a meal. In the afternoon, the crowds in the Market Place were entertained by band concerts. After the reception, the battalion returned to Tidworth. It was from there that it mobilised the following year for the First World War.

The remnants of the 2nd Battalion after the action at Reutel, 24 October 1914. This photograph shows the commanding officer, Lt-Col. Forbes, at the head of what remained of his battalion after being overrun and captured. All these men were regular soldiers, many with service in India, South Africa and Gibraltar. They later became known as The Old Contemptibles. The battalion left England with 1,000 men and thirty officers; by 24 October 450 men and eighteen officers had been captured, seventy-six men and seven officers were killed, 229 men wounded. On 26 October the battalion paraded 250 men and two officers. The men shown in the photograph were to spend four years in captivity. Lt-Col. Forbes was congratulated by the German general on the resistance shown by his battalion, who only capitulated after the final assault by two complete German regiments.

A drawing from a First World War regimental Christmas card. It clearly demonstrates the importance of the regiment's past glories. It is almost as if the baton of regimental history, traditions and Battle Honours – Louisburg, Nive, Peninsula, New Zealand, Ferozeshah, Sobraon, Sevastopol, Pekin 1860, South Africa 1879, South Africa 1900–02 – are being passed on to a new generation. The next four years were to prove a stiff test of the regiment's resolve.

Other titles published by Tempus

Royal Berkshire Regiment 1914–1959
MARTIN MCINTYRE

Through a volatile period in European history the Royal Berkshire Regiment was a bedrock of the British Army. Covering both world wars, this book traces the modern history of this proud regiment, from the outbreak of war in 1914 to its amalgamation with the Wiltshire Regiment in 1959, with a series of photographs that gives a real sense of military life and the spirit of our soldiers during times of conflict and peace.

978 07524 3471 1

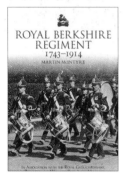

Royal Berkshire Regiment 1743–1914
MARTIN MCINTYRE

This is the prequel book to the Royal Berkshire Regiment 1914–1959. It tells the story of the regiment from its earliest days, looking at its experiences through the American War of Independence, the Napoleonic Wars, the Crimea, Afghanistan 1880 and the Boer War, right up to the outbreak of the First World War. An informative commentary providing an intriguing account of the regiment over this period.

978 07524 3914 6

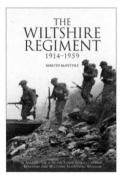

The Wiltshire Regiment 1914–1959
MARTIN MCINTYRE

Focusing on the period between the First World War and 1959, the date of the regiment's amalgamation with the Royal Berkshire Regiment when they formed the Duke of Edinburgh's Royal Regiment (Berkshire and Wiltshire), this painstakingly researched book vividly documents the Wiltshire Regiment's role in many campaigns and battles from the trenches on the Western Front to terrorists in Cyprus in 1959, from Shanghai through to the Second World War.
978 07524 3085 8

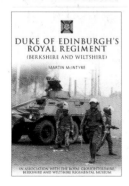

The Duke of Edinburgh's Royal Regiment (Berkshire and Wiltshire)
MARTIN MCINTYRE

The amalgamation of the Royal Berkshire and Wiltshire regiments in 1959 witnessed the formation of the new Duke of Edinburgh's Royal Regiment (Berkshire and Wiltshire). Recruiting heavily from the two counties, it became very much a family regiment and continued to follow the traditions of both its former regiments. This fascinating collection records the actions of the Duke of Edinburgh's Royal Regiment from its beginning in 1959 through to 1994.
978 07524 4178 8

If you are interested in purchasing other books published by Tempus, or in case you have difficulty finding any Tempus books in your local bookshop, you can also place orders directly through our website

www.tempus-publishing.com